The girl with nine toes
Ray Wilkins

We live in a world where human evolution has taken giant steps over the last decades. The Computer, Internet, Video games, iPods and other information and entertainment tools are an everyday part of our private and professional lives. Daily stress and consumption of information is extreme and almost impossible to assimilate into our normal thinking structure. The media bombard us with news and views, images that shock and disturb our inner Balance. Schools are falling apart as they become fortresses trying to protect our children against aggression, anger, injury and even death. Many people have forgotten how it feels to lie down in newly mown grass, beneath the sun, listening to the birds singing and the other soothing sounds of life. We have lost contact to ourselves, to our emotions and to our spirit. This is a story about people finding their way back into the awareness of feeling whole. It is a story about waking up and having the courage to look at life from the inside of the heart. How often do you think back to the past and think "If only I had done that differently!,, Sometimes with regret. Sometimes with sadness and sometimes, even with a feeling of hopelessness. This is a tale about a man who chose to change his way of living. No easy decision for anyone, especially when it means swimming against the current; but, what was that saying? *Only dead fish swim with the current.* I hope that you, the reader will enjoy reading this book and also feel moved to make a change, because I believe that everybody has the power to make a change in his or her life. Just ask yourself—what will change in the future if I do this differently?

Ray Wilkins FRSA Belgium 2007

The girl with nine toes
A story about personal growth
RAY WILKINS

BAREFOOT BOOKS

The girl with nine toes

Manufacture and Publisher
Books on Demand GmbH Norderstedt

Cover design
Christopher Arimont and Cordula Ehms

Artwork
Ray Wilkins "Wild"

ISBN: 978-3-8334-8157-4

BAREFOOT BOOKS

The Barefoot School: College for coaching, training, art
and complementary medicine BCMA. Alte Schule
Weisten B-4791 Burg Reuland, Belgium.
www.thebarefootschool.com

For Cordula
and the girl with nine toes

FOREWORD

It must be one of the great paradoxes of modern times. Choices and personal freedoms abound, at least for the wealthy minority moneyed classes of this increasingly divided world. Cheap air flights, unlimited foreign travel, multiple holidays, unimaginable access to information and communication through the Internet. Freedom, escape and fantasy at every corner, at every turn. Magazines, television and film urge us on to this promised land of luxury, style and excess. Weekend breaks in Dubai?–At your service!

But it comes at a price. This boundless vision of freedom is driven by acquisition, by consumption and by material wealth. It is fuelled by style and brand and conformity. The costs of pollution and the disappearance of nature and the natural world are someone else's problems, not mine. That's progress. But beneath the surface is an anxiety and a level of stress to keep up with modern times, to keep up with the pace. Decisions are rushed, speed is everything, and work is long and hard, but materially rewarding. The prize is the access to the fast lane of modern life. But at what cost?

The Girl with Nine Toes – A Story about Personal Growth' is a parable of our modern times. It is the voice of an old world talking to our new world. It is a voice that starts by asking us to start looking back inside ourselves. Forget the dazzle and the bright lights and the superficialty of modern life. Forget even the anxieties, the

6

stress, the marital breakdowns, the breakdown in communications and emotions between wives and husbands and between parents and their children. Stand back from it all and ask instead different questions–Who am I? Where am I going? Where do I want to go? How will I get there? Who will help me on the journey? Who can I help on my way there?

Like all parables, whether from the Christian gospels or other of the world's great religions, the message is timeless. The story form is deliberate. A parable is not telling you **what** to think but rather to stir the imagination to know **how** to think.

'The Girl with Nine Toes' is a story from an even more ancient world–the aboriginal tradition, the native peoples, not just in Australia as told here but from the First Nations everywhere. These teachers are telling us something about our own survival–but crucially also theirs. Listen well and you shall hear. Hear well and you shall act.

Tony Long
(Director of the WWF European policy office)

7

Down there where the Murrumbidgee flows
Beneath the weeping willow trees and gums
There lives a girl with just nine toes
She's a wild one and lives alone
Among the wallabies under the sun
Unkempt hair from hot winds blown
She knows a lot about them old laws
Set down by the coloured lizard man
Spirits, bunyips and open crocodile jaws
Let her see your eyes and she will look
Into your soul and way beyond
Dreams and things like an open book
The girl with nine toes She knows
She'll tell you to lay down your guns
And fight for peace with your feet
Running to the sun, now take a seat
Look at the world up there on the stage
The players of jealousy hate and rage
Who forget their song lines?
And that love only finds
Her victims in a world of peace
Free of smoke and grey gun grease
Down their where the Murrumbidgee flows
Beneath the weeping willow trees and gums
There lives a girl with just nine toes
And if you asked her for a hand
She will answer with a sardonic smile
How many toes have an angel's hand?
Do you need to seek that girl?
Down their where the war blood flows
Or can you find that missing toe
In your mind deep within
That gives you the answer
In this world to win
Believe in your power
To love your planet
And yourself
Grab it! Grab it!
Your life I mean
With full ten toes, down there where you really care
Where your heart beat freely flows, count your toes!

Chapter 1

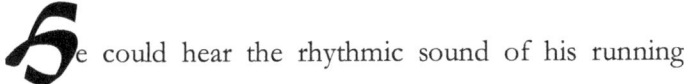e could hear the rhythmic sound of his running shoes whispering across the forest floor. The sun shining through the gum trees sent shadows of light down to play their weird games on the narrow path he was jogging through. He could feel his heart beating faster in his chest and his breath started to slow down as he felt himself slipping into the running flow rhythm to which he was accustomed. Somewhere behind him he could hear the noise caused by his two bodyguards; he could hear them grunting and cursing trying to keep up with him. As he jogged through the trees enjoying this brief feeling of freedom his thoughts wandered back to the events of the day.

The alarm clock started its hysterical screaming at seven o'clock and wouldn't stop until I managed to roll over and press down the button. I had a headache, most probably because of the booze that I drank at the barbecue organised by the Lion's Club last night. I also felt a dark cloud wrapping around my thoughts, a feeling that I've had a lot frequently lately, since Mary died two years ago, actually. I immediately felt the tears coming into my eyes so I quickly swallowed them down with a glass of water and three Aspirin. At the breakfast table I started reading the "Canberra Times" there was a new article about me, discussing about how weak I was, hanging onto the shirt tails of my friends in America, and basically informing the public that I was failing the country, and if something didn't happen soon Australia would become the next third world country. Unemployment was rising and my rate of popularity was sinking. Even my housekeeper kept looking at me through hooded eyes, clouded with disappointment as she was clearing up the breakfast table.

I heard the horn of the car outside in the driveway, it was time to go to work and I only wanted to go back to bed.

On the way to Parliament House I fell asleep in the back seat, but when we stopped at the separate entrance I had my eyes open, ready to seize the day. I walked into my office and started going through my agenda for the day, all the appointments and meetings, pages of information that I had to read through. But all of a sudden I felt dizzy and disoriented. Falling into my chair I took some deep breaths and put my feet up on the desk, and I soon began to feel better; I started my days business.

Somehow everyone I talked to seemed to be boring or I just had the feeling that they were not quite telling the truth I found myself nodding my head saying the proper "yes's," "no's," and "that's interesting," at the proper moments. Everything my eyes saw appeared colourless–almost grey–and there was a feeling of emptiness within my body that I couldn't shake. Maybe I should make an appointment to see Doc Weber *before* my annual check-up comes up. Anyway, I stumbled through the day without making any grave mistakes and now here I am on the banks of the Murrumbidgee getting some exercise and fresh air–trying to find my way back into a life where I can once again feel good about what I am doing.

I kept on running, listening to the sounds of the river and my breathing, when all of a sudden I lost my balance. Falling to the ground, I felt the earth give way beneath my legs and I started sliding down an embankment towards the river, hitting my head on a rock. Everything went black and I heard nothing but silence.

"John, John wake up! It's time for a change, open your eyes!"

This is exactly what I did and I found myself looking into the deepest, blackest eyes I had ever seen in my entire life. The eyes belonged to the face of a very old, black man, wrinkled and scarred, standing naked in the sun, carrying a spear in his right hand; a woomera was hanging from his shoulder. He offered me his arm, and standing shakily with the help of this strange man I asked, "Who the hell are you and what are you doing here? What happened to me? I have a terrible headache and my men are probably searching for me and getting very worried–so if you want to kidnap me do it right now!" The stranger looked deeper into my eyes and passed his right hand slowly in front of my eyes and whispered in a soft, enticing voice

"Let your pain become smoke and your worry a river mist rising in the dawn."

"Hey what was that? My headache's gone and for the first time in months I feel lighter than a sixteen wheeler truck!" The strange man remained silent and turning into the tea tree scrub he beckoned me to follow him. There was a winding path going down to the river and the air started to get cooler. I could feel a light breeze that was scented with wattle. I had no idea where I was going but at the same time I had a feeling of *Déjà vu* – as if I'd already known what was going to happen. Soon we came to the edge of the river and there, sitting on a large rock, was a small Aborigine girl singing softly, trailing her hand in the slowly flowing water. The old man looked into my eyes and said.

"This is the girl with nine toes, she will change your life." Then he simply disappeared. I was shocked and, as if I had been hypnotised, I went to the rock and sat down in front of the girl with nine toes.

"Welcome to my home *Turawwa*–do you want to live or die?"

I looked at her, seeing a face that was full of wisdom and purity and, at the same time, as innocent as a small child's; there was the beginning of a smile on her lips. I stuttered.

"Live of c …c …course."

"Okay *Turawwa,* if you really want to live, you must change many things in your life, especially your thoughts and the things in which you believe. Your very thoughts create your reality whether good or bad." Her voice sounded like singing and I could not see her lips moving; her head was bobbing from side to side and her yellow eyes were shining. Even though I had no idea what was happening, I could remember the stories that the Aborigines told about a girl with nine toes. Stories I had never really believed. I was listening, watching and feeling in awe at what this little girl with nine toes was telling me.

"You are Turawwa, this means *leader of the heart.* You were chosen long ago to lead this country into a future where all people prosper, regardless of their colour or their beliefs. This is your challenge. The way will not be easy and it will take a long time. But first you must decide if you are willing to give everything you have, even your heart, to walk this path. Close your eyes. Go inside and ask your inner self if all parts of you–the inside and outside; the conscious and unconscious of the past, present, and future–are willing to fight together at your side through this life-changing process, to always stand at your side and to support you with all that they have. Yes or no?" I closed my eyes and even though the instructions were strange, I found myself asking all parts of my body if they were willing to support me in what was happening to me–even though I had no idea what it was. I got a load of yes's in reply and a tingling sensation in my belly. I shouted "YES!" and opened my eyes. Then she said;

"There is only one truth and that is the truth in which *you* yourself believe. Your first challenge is to learn to trust your inner self, your intuition, your teacher inside. This may be difficult–there are people out there who do not agree with what you say or what you decide. They will attempt to manipulate you and force you to compromise. They may even try to pressure you with threats or promises. But whatever they say, you must stand up for your own beliefs and decisions, no matter what the consequences are. If you stand like the tall gum tree with your roots firmly planted in the soil of trust within yourself, the winds of change will do the rest!" She then asked me to put my hand on my belly, where I felt the tingling sensation. "This is your center, your place of power and certainty; whenever you feel out of balance or unsure about a decision, place your hand here and feel the warmth. Now imagine forming a connection between your mind and this place, allow yourself to take advice and listen to the voices coming from this part of you, all answers should come from your center. With practise, this will become second nature to you."

I stood up, feeling surprisingly awake and looking down at her feet I could see for the first time that she really did have only nine toes! I heard somebody calling my name. I looked up to the embankment and saw Rick, one of my bodyguards, waving his arms frantically shouting at me to climb out of the gully. I started to say "Wait, I want you to meet the girl with nine toes …!" but when I looked back at the water the rock was empty.

I climbed up to the place where Rick and Joe were waiting for me and told them how I had fallen down the embankment and hit my head. They looked at me in a funny way and Rick said "But there are no scratches or anything, boss and you were only gone for about two minutes anyway-are you feeling alright?"

"I feel better than I've felt in a long time boys, let's go home!"

Believe in yourself, it's worth it!

Chapter 2

John opened his front door and called out to his housekeeper Joan to come into his office. She walked up to him slowly and said. "Yes sir, dinner is almost ready." With her usual sharp, somewhat detached voice. John laid his right hand on his belly, took a deep breath and said "Joan, wait. I don't know exactly what's going on with you or what you really think about me, but over the last two years I can't help feeling that you are pissed off with me about something. I want you to have the courage to tell me what's bothering you. What have I done to upset you?"

Joan's mouth dropped open, she couldn't believe what he had just said. She had been working for this family for over ten years and the Boss had never spoken with her with so much openness and honesty. Why, he even said "pissed off"! Woww ! This was really new. Something could be changing at last. She was thinking as she slowly closed her mouth and started to speak:

"Does this mean that I can say what I really think and feel, even if it may hurt you, sir, and I won't get fired?" John looked straight into her eyes pressed his hand a bit harder on his belly and said, although not quite as clearly as he wanted to. "Yes. My intuition tells me that there is something about me that you don't like and I want to know what that is."

"Okay sir, here I go. As long as I have known you, you were never a person who talked about what he thought, I guess that's why you're a politician, you are always hiding behind your feelings and trying to be bloody diplomatic at the same time. But since Mary ... oh sorry, I mean, Mrs Macmilan died, I have not seen you show any sadness whatsoever. Oh sure! At the Funeral, a controlled tear, here or there, and a timely nose blow when somebody mentioned her name and that was it. Everyday you get up, have a shower, eat breakfast, go to the Parliament building, work, then you come home. You shut yourself in the office together with Mr Glenlivet and then you call that a bloody day. I can't stand it any longer, Mr Macmilan, I have known you, Sarah and Caroline now for over ten years. You have stopped talking to me except for orders and questions concerning the house. When was the last time you hugged one of your daughters and told her that you loved her? When was the last time you showed any kind of feelings towards me or your daughters? Sometimes I have a feeling that this country is being run by a robot, not by a man!"

Her voice was getting louder and her cheeks redder. She was a thin small woman, but at this moment John felt as though she were a giant. Simultaneously, a feeling of sadness and joy began to creep slowly over his body. The tears came hesitantly, at first rolling down his cheeks. He knew that what this simple and homely woman was saying was perfectly true. He had been hiding behind his feelings, afraid to be weak or to express his sadness.

"You are right Joan, thanks for saying that, but could you give me a moment alone? I need to chew over what you've just said—this time without Mr Glenlivet, by the way." She turned towards the door without looking back. She couldn't help but smile after experiencing her boss behaving like a human being.

"Maybe there is still hope for Australia." She whispered to herself.

John sat down with his head hanging and the tears falling onto his trousers. I feel so lost and cold, he thought to himself, almost as if there were a door inside of me that I have yet to open or that I'm afraid of opening. I always thought that I had to protect myself from being hurt and the best way to do that was to close up. Mary was always telling me to talk about my feelings-sometimes she even got frustrated from beating at my closed doors, and there were times when I couldn't even hear her knocking. Sarah and Caroline have even stopped talking to me-apart from mundane phrases like "How's it going dad?" "Have some more mashed potatoes!" or "Dad, can I use the car tonight?"

But they never talked about what was going on inside of them and I have a feeling that we are drifting apart from each other. Today, like some sort of miracle I meet this strange girl down by the river who tells me how to change my life and yeah-it's really funny -but I have a gut feeling that something really important is happening to me, something I can't yet grasp or describe. I'm not even sure if I really believe that she exists.

And yet, when I came home everything looked different, stronger and more intensive. When I saw Joan, I just was not able to close the door-almost as if a little black hand had taken hold of the doorknob and was pulling the door open. I simply have no choice. Or do I?

The tears slowly dried and John, standing up, opened the door to his office and went into the kitchen where dinner was set. In the middle of the table there was a single red rose.

An open heart can change the world

Chapter 3

Thin rays of sunlight were struggling to get through the blinds as John opened his eyes to a new day. *I dreamt about that girl with nine toes almost the whole night,* he thought, while looking at the dressing table where the alarm clock read six thirty. *Wowww! I'm even awake before the alarm has gone off! This is going to be a great day–I can feel it in my toes!*

I was sitting alone at the breakfast table when Sarah and Caroline walked into the dining room. Sitting down carefully in their chairs, they looked warily at me. "Morning dad!" they said in unison "Sleep good?"

"Yeah sure! Except for black hands on door knobs and girls with nine toes I had a great night!,, They looked at each other, half smiling, thinking the same thing.

"Yeah, Joan talked to us last night before we went to bed." said Caroline the eldest of the two.

"And what, may I ask, did nosey Joan say to you about last night?" I asked.

Sarah piped up.

"She said that you've started to open up doors and that's great and if we notice your eyes looking a little bit moist this morning we should keep our mouths shut."

"Joan might be nosey but she is a very wise woman and she's right, except for the part about keeping your mouths shut." I paused for a second, swallowing down

21

my hesitation and then continued. "As of now I want you two girls to talk to *me*. No, not just the everyday stuff, but everything! How school's going? Any new books that you're reading? Do you have boy friends?"

"Dad, I'm only thirteen I haven't even got my period yet!" giggled Sarah.

"I just … I mean … I want us all to talk with each other more than we have been doing lately. I want to get closer to you both. I know my work takes up a lot of my time and I'm often away in other countries, but I want to relate to you both on a more deeper level than just mashed potatoes and car keys." They both laughed. Caroline looked directly into his eyes and said.

"Does this mean that we can even talk with you about Mum?" Her voice was a bit shaky, I felt the corners of my eyes becoming somewhat damp and answered.

"I think it's about time that we talked about *everything*, especially your Mother. I don't know exactly why I'm saying all this, but I'm going through some sort of change in my life and the first thing I've learned is to trust my intuition, to start believing in myself and to stand behind that what I say. This also means talking to you girls about subjects that I generally avoid like your Mother, for example." Sarah and Caroline both stood up, came over to me, and hugged me tight. Caroline said,

"Welcome back to the land of feeling."

Sarah added

"Love you dad! Shit! We have to go or we'll miss the bus!" she shrieked, then they quickly grabbed their school bags and rushed out the back door.

I sat there alone, listening to the birds singing in the trees in the backyard. Looking out the bay window I could see the lawn flowing down to the edge of the lake at the end of the property, a lone swallow flew over the

22

trees and I thought, *We are never alone, as long as we have a memory of someone that brings to us feelings of joy and love. I have a feeling of belonging, belonging to something greater than myself. I want to call it hope! I wonder what the girl with nine toes would say to that?*

He picked up his briefcase as he heard the horn of the car in the driveway.

This world is very friendly...
why aren't we?

Chapter 4

"Mr Prime Minister this just does not work! You cannot punish unemployed people by cutting their benefits just because they don't like working." These words came from one of his main advisors for Social Security, they were sitting in the main conference room and were discussing the unemployment crisis.

"Mr Norton, I will say this only once, and only once, this is *why* we have an unemployment problem. As long as people are fed their unemployment benefit checks every month and at the same time are too lazy to take up a job, whatever it is, even as a garbage man or a cleaning lady then we are just supporting their patterns of laziness.

I know full well that this is a difficult subject, for you and for the rest of the party members, as well as for the people of Australia—but just imagine a nation of people who really enjoy working, who are willing to take risks even if it means starting at the bottom of the ladder again to make their life worth living. Instead of giving them money, let's give them new opportunities to learn a new profession, start up their own business. Let us encourage independence instead of dependence. We have to teach the people what it's like to feel more self-esteem and self-responsibility, to be able to stand up on their own two feet and say *I want to help make this world a better place to live in.* Instead of suffering from feelings of hopelessness and aggression, which are nothing but the seeds of laziness and *No future* consciousness which is developing among our younger people looking for jobs when they leave high school, let's have the courage to make a change!"

There was dead silence in the conference room, thirty eight men and women holding there breath, too surprised to be able to react. Mr Norton packed up his papers stomped out of the room with a look of disgust on his face. Some of the other Members of Parliament (mostly women) stood up and applauded, the rest of the people present were either too astonished or too moved to do anything. That this man, John Macmilan, normally a reserved yes-man, was capable of such strength of character—was hard to digest.

John felt his head getting hot and his face was as red as a tomato, but inside he felt fantastic! At last, he had said what he had thought concerning a major issue, not caring about how anybody else would react, just following his heart. He knew that this was just the beginning of the battle—not just a political battle, no way, this was a personal fight, a fight to find his own inner truth. He looked up at the gallery where there were paintings from Australian artists and his eyes fell on one that he thought, must be new because he had not seen it up till now. It was a painting of an Aborigine standing on a rock pointing in the distance to the horizon, and he looked suspiciously like the old man who had led him down to the river.

A vision is a path...
A guide to your
dreams
Dream your vision
everyday
And it will become a
reality

Chapter 5

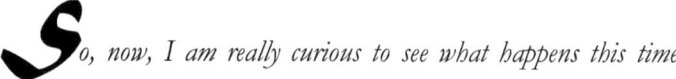*o, now, I am really curious to see what happens this time*

when I go down to the river. I was thinking, while tying up my trainers. The same two bodyguards as yesterday were also getting ready to get onto the jogging path. I couldn't help noticing how they kept looking over their shoulders to see what I was doing. They looked somewhat suspicious - or maybe they just thought I was going crazy. I started doing some stretching exercises and after a few minutes I started slowly jogging down the path. Once again I could feel the wind upon my skin drying the perspiration and I could hear the rhythmic sound of my feet and the calling of the birds in the trees. I could now see the place where I had fallen and without thinking, I turned off the track and slid down into the gully.

"Welcome back into the dreamtime, *Turawwa!*" said the old black man. "Do you have headaches again today?"
"No I don't, old man, but I'd really like to know what your name is?"
"The people call me *Baldwa* which means *the guide*, but we don't have enough time to talk about names now, we have to go, she's waiting, follow me!"
We went down the same path and I had the same feeling of temperature change; all sound simply vanished.

I had a feeling we were walking into a vacuum, where time did not exist. Baldwa turned his head and, leaning on his spear, stopped and pointed to the opening in the bushes where I could see the Murrumbidgee flowing.

"She is there, go and get a change!" I blinked and he was gone. I walked down to the river and there she sat on the same rock in the same position with the same half-smile touching her lips.

"Welcome back, Turawwa; sit down and listen. You are walking well on your path and the next challenge which awaits you will bring you even closer to yourself. Having a vision is like turning on a light. At this moment, you can see with the eyes of your mind the place where you want to go. You may call this your dream, your goal. Holding this vision inside your head will give you the power to keep going, regardless of the difficulties you will experience. This is your motor, driving you forward into the future. Now close your eyes and see within the path leading into the future. Do you notice the direction in which it flows? Is it as a silver river? Or a road leading over the mountains? As you allow this path to become clearer in time, imagine being able to see your vision floating back to where the path ends. Looking back, you are able to see and understand the many different steps that you took on this path, in time, to reach this goal, but as well as this, and even more important, you need to recognise the challenge that you faced before you took the next step, and to know how you did that exactly? What did you change? What exactly did you win when you made that step? And what exactly had changed in your life? Asking these questions brings you closer to your vision and gives you the answers to questions that you will face in the future. Be clear about which steps you take and whom you take with you. Notice which inner feelings inside of you, move you the most. Now imagine yourself standing on the bank of a wide river, on the other bank of this river you can see your vision. Yes! Not only can you see it, you can even hear the noises and voices that go together with this vision, you can feel it inside yourself, even taste and smell it. Your future, your goal. Now in order to cross to the other bank you have to use the stepping stones that you have laid out for yourself in the water. Take the first step only when you know you are ready."

Listening to the sing-song rhythm of her voice I found myself going into something like a trance. I could actually see the river in my imagination. The colours were really intense and all noises were incredibly clear. I could see myself jumping to the first stone and I shouted out loud: "*Courage!*" And the girl with nine toes looked up at me and said "You have now reached your first stepping stone on your way to true leadership, now go back into your country and practice what you have learnt!"

"Mr Macmilan, Mr Macmilan, Sir, where are you?" I could hear them shouting from up on the jogging path, I leapt up the embankment and almost bumped into Rick

"Here I am, men, let's get back to moving the world!" They both looked at each other with that queer look they both had, and then, shrugged there shoulders and we all started jogging back to the car.

Have the courage to speak up
and know love

Chapter 6

*J*ohn opened the front door and called out to his daughters "Sarah, Caroline where are you two? Come down here, I want to talk with you both!"

They sat around the kitchen table, all three looking a little bit uncomfortable. Joan made everything a little bit merrier by breezing into the kitchen to make herself a cup of tea.

"I want to start a new realationship with the both of you. Well, actually the three of you!" He said looking up at Joan, who was standing by the stove.

" I know that I have been closed for a long time now—even at work it's the same, I can function, I can even make decisions, I can talk to people but I've forgotten how to show my feelings. It sometimes feels as though there were a band of steel wrapped around my heart." He felt his eyes getting watery again, *damn that girl!* Well to make it brief, I've decided to have the courage to start opening up to all of you. I don't really know how to do it, but I have met a girl with nine toes whose showing me how to jump onto stones."

"Dad! Wait! Wait! What are you talking about girls with nine toes and jumping on stones? Hee?"

John took a very deep breath and then started to tell the three of them all about his visits to the girl at the river, leaving nothing out. When he had finished, to his amazement, there were no looks of disbelief to be seen. Joan even asked if she could come next time too, maybe Baldwa could cure the warts on her feet and heal her Varicose veins. They all laughed heartily and John felt lighter than he had ever felt in a long, long time.

Live your dreams

Chapter 7

e was lying in bed and listening to the songs of the crickets outside in the garden; his thoughts started slipping back into the past as he remembered moments, both professional and personal, when he had not had the courage to say what he was really thinking or feeling. Looking at the scenes flashing in front of his eyes, he could see how the decision to not say what he thought or what his intuition suggested, resulted only in feelings of anger, sadness or frustration. He suspected that he seldom got what he really wanted anyway, because he was afraid of hurting somebody's feelings, afraid that he might be wrong or just plain too lazy to open up his mouth. Then he saw an image in the darkness that looked something like Mary's face trying to tell him something–it sounded like *follow your heart*. Well, that's almost sure to be something that the girl with nine toes would have said, he thought, as he slowly drifted off to sleep.

Love yourself and the world will
love you

Chapter 8

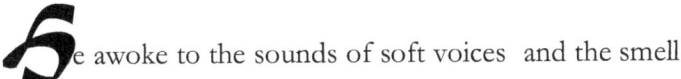e awoke to the sounds of soft voices and the smell

of a cooking fire. He opened his eyes, he could see a low roof made of what looked like bark and branches. He was in some kind of hut and somebody was calling out his name, "Turawwa!Turawwa! The sun is waiting! come outside and seize the day!" He crawled out of the hut to see a group of Aborigines sitting around a fire drinking tea, a large black billy can was hanging over the fire. He walked up to the circle and sat down, an old woman who was tending the fire gave him a mug of tea, it tasted sweet and strong but it went down good. A man with feathers stuck all over his body said:

"Turawwa you have now reached the second stone crossing the river, this is the lesson of *self-trust*. There is absolutely no one in this world who you can completely trust, except yourself. How can you look inside the heads of people to see if they are telling the truth or if they carry the spear of integrity? But you can look inside of your own mind and heart to understand the songs the ancestors are singing for you. In every situation where you have to make a decision, even if the consequences may be dangerous or may hurt somebody else, even

37

someone you love–you must follow your heart This is the path of excellence."

My eyes started to water, but this time because of the smoke of the fire and I answered: "I think I am ready to jump to the second stone, but I am afraid of failing as I have often done in the past." I took another swallow of the sweet tea and looked across the fire at the man with many feathers. He responded:

"Think back to a time in the past when you were confronted with a big problem, when you had to make a decision alone, without the help or advice from anyone else. And the decision you made was perfect, even though it was difficult to carry out. How did you feel at this moment, knowing that *this was right?*"

I thought of a time when I had to make a decision concerning sending troops to the Timor region. Everyone was against it, but I wanted to fight for peace. As I was imagining myself standing alone and knowing without any shadow of doubt that the decision was right, I could see myself standing up straight, with my shoulders relaxed and a slight smile on my lips. There was a warm deep feeling inside my chest and, when I put my hand onto this place, the feeling became even stronger.

"This is your moment of *excellence*, use this power song every time you have to make a decision. If you do not experience it, then the decision is not right." said Mister Feathers.

I opened my eyes to look around at the other people but to my amazement, I was sitting alone at the fire and all I could see was a flat, dusty stretch of earth dotted with stumpy, gnarled bushes and some dried up patches of grass. I stood up and looked up at the sun: it was hot, even though it must still have been early in the morning. I could hear voices coming from the nearby

38

scrub and all of a sudden two children, a boy and a girl, ran out towards where I was standing. The girl said: "The girl with nine toes sent me to give you the new challenge. In order to help you on your way, I will do all that I can to assist you. I am on your side!" Her voice sounded quite soothing and kind, but for some reason she wouldn't look me directly in the eye.

"My name is Wootara and this is Yarawwa." said the other child, a scruffy looking boy of about twelve.

"You have to decide which one of the two of us you can trust to be your guide–and you have to decide fast!" He explained, sounding very brusque and impatient. He looked straight into my eyes without a trace of a smile on his face. I had known situations like this very well in my past when faced with having to decide which person was right and which one was wrong. Most of the time, I tended to believe that the person who was polite and nice towards me was the person to trust; sometimes, it even went so far that I was afraid of hurting feelings if I said 'no' to someone. I looked at the girl and went inside to feel what my heart said. She smiled at me and batted her eyelids. I felt nothing. I looked at the boy; he looked right at me. I put my hand over my heart and it felt warm and strong. I declared, "It is you that I want, Wootara!" and Yarawwa just disappeared.

Wootarra turned towards the dessert and mumbled something that sounded like "*follow me*!" And I followed. It was getting hot and I started to sweat, the sand squeaked beneath my bare feet and all I could hear was the silence of the desert but, after a while, Wootara stopped in his tracks "Listen Turawwa, *leader of the heart,* what do you hear?"

I closed my mouth and my eyes and concentrated on listening. After a while, I could hear what sounded like very faint voices coming from a long distance."These are the voices of the ancestors connected to your inner voice, of whom you can ask any question, anytime, wherever you are. Here lies all the information and all the answers you will ever need to be happy and successfull–but the only way to be able to truly hear the voices is to listen with your heart."

One smile can move a mountain

Chapter 9

I opened my eyes to the light coming through the curtains. I could see tiny dust devils dancing in the sunlight. I didn't move a muscle because I was afraid I would forget the dream. The images were still strong in my memory, as well as Wootara's voice, and what he had said. I got out of bed, opened the curtains, then the window, and breathed in the fresh morning air. I was deeply aware of the outside world, something I had not felt since I was a child running wild around the homestead where I had grown up. I walked out onto the grass barefoot, feeling the morning dew on the grass. I could smell the freshly cut grass and, somewhere high up in the gum trees, I could hear a kookaburra laughing. I was thinking that I had a lot to learn. Many times in the past, I had not listened to my heart. Mary was always telling me to trust my intuition, to speak straight from the gut! This was actually an argument that kept coming up in our relationship whenever we had to make some kind of decision concerning the family. At work, I hardly ever made a lightning, impulsive decision. Some of my aides had even given me the nickname Macsnail. I needed tons of information, answers to all the questions. I hardly ever took enough time to find the answers for myself. Wait a minute! Isn't that what Wootara said last night in the dream? This inner voice. Some kind of connection to the ancestors.

I came out of the clearing onto the edge of the lake, my pajamas cuffs started to get heavy and wet but I sat down on the grass anyway, something I would never do normally, unless I had first laid out a blanket and checked for ants. I looked out at the water. The mist was slowly rising off the still water and I could smell that mildewy scent of the lake. Looking out onto the water I noticed the colours changing as the sun rose over the hills on the other side of the lake. I could feel a strong connection to the earth, reminding me of what a beautiful place we lived in-and I started humming that old Loius Armstrong song "It's a Wonderful World".

"Mr Macmilan, Mr Mac', breakfast is ready!" I could hear Joan shouting from the veranda, so I left Mr Armstrong to look after his part of the world, stood up, stretched my body and walked towards the house to start to look after my part of the world.

Hate is a feeling that stems from fear

Chapter 10

I now invite all citizens of this country to take their futures into their own hands. This government believes in self-responsibility and in the Power of Hope. From this day on, all social benefits for unemployed persons will be reduced by forty per cent. Each person regardless of gender, colour, or religion is now legally able to work as an independent agent in their own business even if they are currently employed. All otherwise unemployed persons will now work at least six hours per day in a social/medical area. For example in hospitals, homes for the aged, meals on wheels, community care centers, environmental projects, feeding the disabled, building roads in the outback, caring for the animals and the land in which we live. If we all work together and give all we have, then, and only then do we have a chance to turn the course of this country from a failing democracy based on dependence and social instability toward a vision where we can be proud to be able to call ourselves Australians.

I was wondering what the girl with nine toes would have said to this statement, when Mrs Simmons, my secretary, asked me if that was the end of the public statement, as she needed to finish typing it up in order to send out the copies to the House of Representatives and it was almost four o'clock. I looked at her face and, for the first time in five years of working together with her, I noticed that she had incredibly warm deep, green eyes and a small scar above her left eyebrow; she was smiling.

45

"Why are you smiling Mrs Simmons?" I asked.

"Sir, if I may be so bold, I have been working in the public service for many years and I have seldom heard such a bold challenging statement concerning employment such as this. I don't know how Mr Norton or the rest of the cabinet will react but I just want to say that I think it's great, sir!" She lifted her ample body out of the chair, closed her laptop and walked out of my office, leaving behind that scent of lavender and old roses that always reminds me of Mary's mother. I leaned back into my chair thinking about the difficulties in changing the laws and regulations concerning the measures for improving employment when all of a sudden I realised what I had just thought. Laws and regulations concerning the measures to improve employment. In political and public language, these were called the laws governing unemployment. Saying this positively, turning it around to something motivating, at least on a semantic level it changed the meaning completely. Miss nine toes again, I guessed. The red light on my telephone was blinking on my private line; I picked up the receiver.

"John? Here's Brian how about coming out to Red Hill tonight for dinner? I haven't seen you in ages mate, do you have time?"

"Brian! Great to hear you, sounds good! Around about eight, okay for you? I'll bring a bottle of red with me if you do the steaks."

"No prob's my friend then uh ... see ya later, alligator." Then he hung up. I couldn't help smiling at the thought that a man—the chief of financial affairs in the Australian government with years of experience in handling huge banks and mega business corporations—could still be so corny.

I didn't have the time to go jogging, but I had a feeling that it was important to meet Brian. We hadn't seen each other in a long time and the girl with nine toes apparently had other ways of changing my thoughts, anyway .

Back home I quickly showered and changed, I met Sarah and Caroline in between putting on my shoes and going down to the cellar to get a bottle of Barossa Valley red wine. I couldn't help thinking about how they had changed–or was it the other way around? At any rate, they seemed so grown up all of a sudden.

Life is to be enjoyed
With every day
With every smile
With every tear

Chapter 11

I drove up into the driveway once again, amazed at the beauty of this house and the surrounding gardens. Old chestnut trees shaded the drive up to the house. Wattle trees and Banksia bushes were planted at strategic spots, apparently following the Chinese philosophy of Feng Shui as Consuela, Brian's wife, had once said. The grass was natural bush grass mixed with dandelions and red poppies and I could see a group of ghost gums shimmering behind the chestnut trees. The whole landscape looked and smelled like well-controlled Australian bush country. The house was a renovated homestead with an outside terrace on all four sides, with old red roof tiles and hortensia vines clinging to the walls; I was really looking forward to dinner with one of my best friends.

"John! Great to see you mate, come out to the back, I've got the barby going and the steaks are already on the grill."

I could see his blue eyes glinting in the evening sun and, with lots of backslapping and shacking of hands, I gave him the bottle of wine and followed him through the hall into the backyard.

"Can I help you Brian? Where's Consuela?"

"I sent her out to ladies night at the club so that we two could be alone, yeah! Go and get the baked potatoes out of the Aga in the kitchen, you know where everything is!"

We sat down and started loading salad onto our plates, the smell of baked potatoes with fresh sage and thyme was making my mouth water. He poured out the wine and said. "Bottoms up!" I laughed for about the tenth time that evening and we started getting tucked in to our dinner. After a few minutes he looked at me in and, in a rare serious moment, said, "John, I've been hearing some funny things about you lately."

"From our friend James Norton, am I right?"

"Yeah, that's right! But you know how he is, he's sometimes loud and belligerent but his heart and wallet are in the right place. Anyway, he said that somehow you have changed, that you're more–how did he say it now, um ... more philosophical ...talking about forcing people to work and only paying people who want to work -you know how he is. He hangs onto the old laws and doesn't like changing his spots. He also said that you're more decisive, and well, he even called you a little Hitler!"

I laughed, almost spilling my wine onto the white linen table cloth that Consuela insists we use even if we are simply enjoying a barbecue.

"Yes Brian, he's right, I am changing, I'm beginning to realise a lot of mistakes that I've made in the past. I think that after Mary died, a part of myself died with her and, because of this, I've become lazy and careless in my job. I have become almost dependent on the decisions and ideas of my aides and assistants. I have lost some of my self-esteem. I know, you've known me now since high school and you know that I was always a good leader. Remember our rugby team, when I used to be the captain and you were playing left wing? Anyway–to get back to the subject–to be a good leader , I had to learn to push down my feelings, to be disassociated from emotions. Over the years of being a politician, somewhere along the line, I had lost contact with myself-with my inner self, do ya' know what I mean?"

"Oh no John! Don't tell me your're going to be one of those Osho followers and start wearing orange overalls!" He laughed.

I felt angry and misunderstood.

"Jesus Brian! For once in your life, be serious and listen to what I'm saying, will you?!" I was pissed off. "I am being manipulated inside my own house, people are using me for their own political goals, the country is falling apart and I'm still mourning my wife instead of doing what I do best–lead! I noticed that he had stopped drinking his wine and, at least, he now looked a little bit more serious and attentive to what I was saying. "And I have also met someone—the girl with nine toes!" He coughed into his glass this time spilling wine onto the white tablecloth. The drops looked like rubies tossed carelessly across the table.

"John, are you telling me that you have a girlfriend and that she's responsible for your psychological cleansing? Who is she? What's her name? No! It's not Mrs Simmons, is it?"

"Brian. Please. Listen very closely. This girl is not a girl, she's like a teacher and she has an uncanny way of getting inside my head and not inside my trousers! Let me try to explain." So, for the second time and what would not be the last time, I explained to a person I loved what I was experiencing, leaving nothing out, I even told him about my nightly dream challenge path. I looked over at him and could see two small tears pushing their way out of the corners of his eyes, he stared at me after I'd finished and after a few minutes of silence he started to speak. "Absolutely, bloody amazing John! Unbelievable! Do you think she knows anything about the stock exchange? Struth! There I go again every time I get emotional I start making jokes. No, seriously as your best friend I have noticed you changing over the last few years. I won't say Mary's death is solely responsible. You were never a person who showed much of his feelings; but since then, you have been more withdrawn and subdued, I was even going to advise you to go back to that psychotherapist who helped you over the initial mourning phase. But it looks like the girl with nine toes beat me to it. I can't say that I understand what it's really all about, but I do know that you are changing for the good. The mere fact that you shouted at me when I wasn't listening to you is a good sign. But tell me now, what are you and this girl planning for Australia?"

"I went through all the ideas that I had inside my head. Lowering the social benefits. Decreasing taxes for new and small businesses, as well as for larger enterprises so that they had more finances to employ more people. The new ideas and innovation programme. An equal rights bill and the environmental projects, everything, every vision that I've ever had since becoming a politician. At the end I felt completely drained, but at the same time elated, especially when my old friend, who knew so much about money and politics, agreed with everything I had said.

"John, this vision will change the face of Australia! And I will do all that I can to support you even if it means kicking Norton in his rearend. Let's have a drink and cheers to that girl waiting for you on the banks of the Murrumbidgee and to a new future for this country!"

We clicked our glasses together, hugged each other like two bears who had just caught and eaten a giant salmon: proud, defiant and boys!

Much later we walked together to my car where the driver was leaning on the hood smoking a cigarette. The air was still and the only sound was the chirping of the crickets and our footsteps on the gravel, opening the passenger door I turned to him and said "I love you, my friend!"

He responded, "Now don't go all gushy on me, John!" I laughed and thought back to what he must have said at least a thousand times in the past about himself *"Whenever I get emotional, I make jokes."*

Trust yourself and your world
will change

Chapter 12

*T*he moment my head touched the pillow, I fell asleep and the first thing I saw was Wootara's small wiry body crouched under the shade of a coolibah tree.

"Turawwa, there you are, we have been waiting for you!" Sitting beside him was a small scraggy bush dog that looked suspiciously like a cross between a dingo and a fox terrier.

"This is Bongo, he will help us today!" With that he jumped up, motioned for me to take the lead and off we went into the burning country. Everything was yellow, orange or white, broken only by the brown, black colour caused by the shadows of a rock or a tree. The land was flat and hot—full of dust, sand, and the occasional kangaroo. I soon realised that I could walk, close my eyes and at the same time listen to my new *inner voices.*

You are the leader, but also the healer—believing in yourself will give you the strength to know which direction to take. Your intuition is your inner teacher. Your challenge is to bring this boy and his friend back to his family who dwell behind the great Red Rock—follow the path of your heart. All of a sudden, I turned to the west and started running, looking back to make sure Wootara and Bongo were following me. Then, all I did was follow my intuition, turning when I knew that it was right, slowing down or running faster or sometimes even stopping to let the other two catch up with me. Every now and then I stroked Bongo's dried up ears and asked him if I was on the right track. If he licked my hand I knew I was right and I wondered if he would bite my hand if I was wrong .

We seemed to have been running for hours, when, all of a sudden, high on the horizon, I could see a huge red rock sitting all alone in the open country. Then I knew I was bringing my two friends back to the right place–their home. Behind the rock, there was a small camp with a few scattered bark and wattle lean-tos, a fire, and a man sitting next to the fire who stood up and waved his arms–it was the feathered man.

"Turawwa, you have jumped the second stone!" He shouted.

As I ran up to the fire, Wootara pulled on my shirt-tail so that I had to turn around. Taking my hands into his small bony hands and looking deep into my eyes he told me,

"Thank you for bringing me home"

"But you said *you* were my guide, and yet, you and Bongo followed *me* the whole time."

"We simply guided you to lead with your intuition and you found the right path using trust," he answered in his gruff, impatient voice. "Now I give you over to my Father."

I took a step towards the fire where Mr Feathers was standing. He clapped his hands once and I opened my eyes hearing somewhere in the distance a dog barking.

Have the courage to be different

Chapter 13

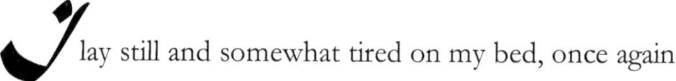

lay still and somewhat tired on my bed, once again remembering every second of the living dream. And knowing deep within myself that what I was learning was more than just learning. This was knowing. Knowing myself. And every step I was taking was a step nearer to my spirit, the part of me that I had forgotten and the part that I remember Mary mentioning many years ago, when she said: *"The part of you that I love the most is your spirit and one day you will get to know this part of yourself; then you will know that you are going home."*

Too many times, especially in my relationship with Mary, I had never really said what I felt. Honesty was a rarity only to be enjoyed when I was sure that I would not hurt anybody and also not be hurt myself. I remember reading somewhere about the idea of *hard love*, which means saying what you think or feel, even if it's going to hurt someone. All of a sudden, I had the urge to drive down to the river, I needed to talk with that girl.

True love is a state of reality, not
a
goal

Chapter 14

*B*aldwa was waiting for me. He took my hand and led me down the path to the river. He looked at me with those piercing black eyes and said. "Enjoy the change!" And then he just disappeared as always.

"Ah! Turawwa, come and sit down. You have been learning a lot, as I have heard from the dreamtime people. Come–sit and listen. I want to talk to you about your next jumping stone. This is the stone of love, but not as you know love. Real love, that survives, is based on the belief that the only true realationship is the realationship with yourself. To be able to really love another person is only possible when you first love yourself. Many people feel weak or incomplete in their lives and are always on the hunt for someone to make them strong, to make them whole again; consequently, they always seek out those partners who are able to fullfill this pattern. This is not love, this is slavery, this is dependence. When two people meet and already feel whole and strong within themselves and also know that they are their own personal leaders, as well as decision makers–if these two people rise in love with each other, then their *realationship* is based on freedom and independence. This is true love. If you look at the forest you will see many different trees living together: gum trees, jacarandahs, wattle, ironbark, banksia bushes and the tea-tree. All these trees are different and every root system is independent from the other roots. Every tree stands alone, only the branches and leaves touch each other, dancing together in the wind, enjoying the freedom of self-responsibility. So, go now and jump to your next stone, Turawwa, and change to enjoy!"

I wanted to ask her a hundred questions but she looked up at me and, with a small impatient wave of her hand, she signalled me to be on my way. I turned around and there stood Baldwa, waiting to lead me once again onto that now familiar path up the ravine to the track going back to where I had parked the car. I drove home slowly, carefully using only the main roads, avoiding any contact with people. I felt like a kid smoking my first cigarette behind the back fence, hidden from the windows of the homestead so that my parents couldn't see me. I know that being out alone without my bodyguards was dangerous but at the same time I was enjoying myself for a change. As I climbed out of the car, I looked at my watch. It was still early, so I had time to sit down to breakfast with the girls.

"Dad, have you been out without the boys?" asked Sarah with a twinkle in her eye and a smile on her face.

"Mind your own business, kid!" I laughed, roughing up her pitch black hair that was shining in the morning sun. Caroline came out of the kitchen onto the terrace. She was wearing jeans and a t-shirt that used to belong to her Mother. I couldn't help thinking about how much she looked like Mary: the same eyes, the same hair, the same body build. I felt that tight feeling around my heart that I always have whenever I think about her.

61

"Hi Dad! Rick and Joe are really pissed off that you went out on your own–they want you to phone them when you get in."

"Yeah, I'll speak to them later, but now, to get back to you two darlings. You have to put up with me for the whole day, so, what do you want to do to prevent the day being boring? Go for a swim? Play tennis? Go for a drive to Mt Stromlo to see the observatory? We'll be together with my two brawny friends, of course. Or shall we just stay here and–how do you say it, Caroline … uhm chill out?"

"How about we just spend a day in the past talking about you and Mum–what happened between you two– and all that stuff. Let's just hang out together and exchange war stories like you and Brian say you always do."

Sarah nodded, and added:

"This is the first time in a long time that we've been together as a family–I really don't know if I can handle it."

"I could see her eyes starting to get misty, but then she jutted out her chin, squared her little shoulders and with much enthusiasm started buttering a piece of toast.

After breakfast we walked together down to the lake and sat down on the cool grass. Looking out at the water I could see bubbles rising to the surface, I wondered if it was a fish or a yabbie lurking below the surface. Caroline spoke up: "Dad, tell us again about what happened between you and Mum, nobody really told us the truth. You didn't talk much anway. Mum was always jumping between hating your guts or sticking up for you and Joan just kept saying everything would be alright–but what really happened?"

I felt myself withdrawing into that space where I felt like closing all those doors against the past as well as against the future, when all of a sudden, inside my head, I heard that strange, soft sing-song voice belonging to the girl with nine toes *"follow your heart and trust."*

"Well, girls, what I'm about to tell you now might be upsetting for you, but I believe that it is well past the time for you both to know how things happened; then, maybe, you can learn something that you might be able to use in your own realationships in the future so that you don't make the same mistakes."

I could see them looking at each other, each involved in her own thoughts, I had a feeling that they were afraid and hopeful at the same time. I went on talking. "At that time, I was busy putting together a new cabinet and was also travelling often to New York for the UN meetings concerning Irak. If you remember, it was about four years ago, I was hardly ever at home. Anyway, your mother and I started arguing a lot. Well, not really arguing—more like she was angry and frustrated and told me in no uncertain terms what she felt. I simply suffered in silence. I guess that's what most men do, when confronted with a crisis in their relationships."

He closed his eyes and, going back into the misty past, he started to put the story together as he had experienced it, trying to put himself into Mary's mind as well as into his own. The images returned, images that he had blocked out over the last two years, images that still caused pain and hurt him even more, because he hadn't had the courage to look at them again, until now.

Be the mountain
Be the ocean
Be the tree
Be happy
Be the light
Be the shadow
Be the rain
Be you
Be

Chapter 15

"John, I know what sort of pressure you are under, you don't have to tell me and, by the way, I'm no stranger to stress and pressure either. I'm only asking you to take a look at what's happening to our relationship. You, me and the family. When was the last time you did something together with the girls? When was the last time we went out together? Now don't start arguing about security sanctions and all that shit, that didn't bother you in the past, sneaking out with me to some dark Italian restaurant incognito or driving up to Lake Eucumbene to do some clandestine fishing at our log house. When was the last time we slept with each other?"

I felt terrible even though I know she was right, but how could I change how I felt? It was as if there was a wall between her and me. I could hear her voice, I could hear her talking, I could even smell that perfume that normally drives me crazy, but I could not tell her what was going on inside of me. Damned if I even knew what was going on inside of me!

"Mary listen, I know what you're feeling, I really do!"

"Oh! So, now you're not only the prime minister of Australia—your'e also a mind reader!"

"No, I'm only trying to tell you how I feel about the situation,"

"Then talk about your own emotions, not mine!" she shouted. I could see the look in her eyes and the way her lips became hard and narrow when she was angry. I knew that this was escalating and getting worse. I looked at my watch and saw that I was late for the next appointment and this, of course, tipped the scales.

"Okay, okay! I can take a hint, John. You don't have any time for me! Well, maybe I just don't have enough time for you either–have a great day!" As she turned towards the door, I felt her hair brushing my face. She slammed the door to my office and I could hear her high heels receding down the corridor. I closed my eyes and tried to pull myself together to be ready for the next Parliamentary meeting.

Mary walked out to her car and after unlocking the door she sat in the driver's seat and took some slow, deep breaths, trying to relax with the exhale–an exercise she learned many years ago when she used to teach Aikido. But it did not seem to be working she thought. Probably works for everybody else, just not for me. Why doesn't he understand what's going on? I love him so much, and I'm sure that he loves me too, but he's so stuck in his work cycle and does not do anything to climb out. Yeah, okay, he was always a little bit heavy. On the one hand such a fantastic politician: successful, loved by the people, a real mover. On the other hand stuck in his feelings, or should I say non-feelings. I often see him being manipulated by some of his advisors and cabinet members and instead of trusting his own intuition and believing in himself, he allows himself to be manipulated. I know that he's also suffering because of this distance between us, but I'm not his therapist and I need all my energy to run our home, get the kids to school and at the same time get my work done at the office. But it's no use complaining, I've got work to do!

She drove onto the main road, in the direction of the law offices of Grant and Garvey where she worked as an associate partner in corporate law.

As she walked into her office, Sharon, her personal secretary called out to her: "Mary! Mr Garvey wants to see you in his office right away." Mary turned to the right and knocked on the heavy, oak door of her boss's office.

"Mary how's it going? Everything hunky dory?" She moaned, she loved her boss, but if there was one thing she couldn't stand about him, it was his use of slang.

"Fine, thanks Tom, and how are you?"

"Everything up to scratch, Mary. I guess you are wondering why I wanted to speak with you. It's like this: we have a proposition to make to you. As you know old Patrick is going into retirement next month and you know that we are on the lookout for a new partner. Anyway, to come to the point, we want to offer you a full partnership in the firm with all fringe benefits, of course. You don't have to sign away your life straight away. Think about it, talk to John about it, and let me know your decision tomorrow morning. And now, get back to your office and earn us some dollars!"

She walked into her office and fell into her chair, feeling speechless and elated.

John said. "Mary that's fantastic! I hope you're going to say yes."

"To be honest, John I don't really know if I have enough energy and time. Especially with the girls. They

67

really need the quality time that I give them now and being a partner means more working hours. Some of it I can do in my office at home, but there are always so many conferences and meetings where I'll have to be present."

"Maybe we can talk to Consuela, she really likes looking after the girls, she thinks of them as her own half daughters–and you know, she and Brian are not able to have any children of their own. She might really like to do some mothering on the side!"

"John! Always the politician! Okay, I'll ring Consuela and if she's willing to spend more time with Sarah and Caroline and if Sarah and Caroline agree, I'll do it."

John's voice sounded softer as he continued telling his two daughter's the story about how their Mother became so successful in her work. And the price that he and she had to pay: distance and acceptance of the situation, even if that meant that their time and love for each other was becoming less and less.

"Our arguments became even more frequent and louder. Deep inside I knew that we were sliding towards disaster. I also knew deep within my heart what it would take to change the situation. If we could only have just put aside the blame and the fear that we both felt and looked at each other with new eyes–aware of what we were creating–we may have discovered solutions to all the problems we had.

Everytime I came home I could see you two trying to be brave and not show your feelings. Your Mother was doing everything she possibly could to hold everything together and all I could think about was saving Australia from financial doom." John looked at the two girls sitting on the grass, watching him with moist eyes. He could see the sadness, but also felt the anger behind the tears–something that he had never been able to feel in the past. He looked out at the ripples on the water and continued talking.

"Your mother started losing weight and was often complaining about feeling really exhausted. During her annual medical check - up they found the lump in her left breast–and this little lump changed our lives. We tried to shield you both from what was going on. The word 'cancer' was forbidden, never to be articulated in your presence. We even coached Joan, who's not used to keeping her mouth shut, not to tell you two anything. All we said was that she was ill, but everything will be alright. This worked until her hair started falling out, as a result of the chemotherapy. Then you, Caroline started to understand what was going on. Do you remember what you said when you realised what was really happening?"

"I think I said something like, 'Mum, please don't leave us alone with Dad.'"

"Yeah, that's right, honey and that hurt me more than I could ever say, I think. The thought that your Mum could die and that you, Sarah and I would keep on living without her–without hearing her voice, without smelling her perfume, without seeing her running down to the lake–was unbearable. Lying alone in bed without feeling the warmth of her body, but also the thought that you and Sarah were afraid of being alone with me, was devestating."

"Dad, no! That's not right! I wasn't afraid of being alone with you. It was just the thought that both saving the world **and** looking after Sarah and me, was too much for you. You got it all wrong!" John looked at his older daughter and felt terrible.

"And all this time, I thought that you thought that I wasn't capable of looking after you, and that you were afraid of me for some reason. Why didn't you tell me all this earlier?"

"We couln't talk to you normally, Dad. You were always busy, tired, or all closed up. Sarah and I felt lost and alone. Yeah, sure, Joan was always there, but she's not our Dad, is she?" John thought back to other times in the past when he hadn´t really listened to, or understood what his daughters were trying to tell him, as well as the situations when he had not understood Mary for the same reasons.

ε – motions move the world

Chapter 16

Mary was lying alone in her bed in the cancer clinic in Sydney. She was hooked up to the chemotherapy infusion. She was angry, sad and lonely all at the same time. He's done it again! She thought to herself. Every time he comes in, I try to talk to him about the future–about what he should prepare himself for, in case I die; about all the feelings that I have and what's going on inside my mind–and what does he do? He turns himself off and pours candy sugar over the pile of shit so that he doesn't have to look at what is really going on. I love him so much, but I feel so helpless, and when I look into his face and see that he's too afraid to look inside at his own feelings and take responsibility for the changes happening. I wish to God that he would learn to find himself again. He looks like a tired broken man, but when I see him on TV giving interviews, he gives the impression that he's fine and has everything under control. She felt tired, she closed her eyes and she soon fell asleep.

"Mary! Mary! Open your eyes, open your eyes!" Mary opened her eyes and found herself sitting on a rock at the bank of a river. It looked like the Murumbidgee, where she and John used to go fishing together. There was a young Aborigine girl with strange eyes and a half-smile on her face sitting beside her: "I am the girl with nine toes and I am here to help you. You know that you will soon step over the border into dream country and I know that you are afraid about what will happen to your husband and children in the future when you are no longer in the land of light." Mary was amazed by the fact that this small, strange creature who called herself the girl with nine toes knew so much about her innermost thoughts. She couldn't help herself to look down at her feet to see if it was really true. And then she remembered what she and John had talked about years ago in Coober Pedy.

"I will bring your husband back to the spirit. This will take many seasons and he must pass though many challenges, but because of these changes in his belief system, his realationship with your two daughters will become deeper and more loving. In fact, he will become even more aware of his power to love and he will have the courage to once again be able to show his feelings.

We need you to forgive John for the pain he caused you. This does not mean that he is absolved or that he is innocent; all it means, is that you are able to let go of your anger and frustration, so that you will once again feel the lightness of the eagle flying–enabling you to fly to the other side in freedom and purity. Above all, know that we will be there to give John all the support he needs to become the leader of the heart. We also ask you to hold this dream inside your heart without telling John. Be free, Be the light, Be the joy!"

Mary could hear the soft beeping sound of the infusomat running her medication. She was trying to understand the meaning of what she had just heard when she turned her head slowly towards the door to see John

73

walking in. He sat down in the plastic chair beside her bed and took her hand in his.

"John, I want to talk with you and I want you to listen to what I have to say: no arguments, no defending yourself, no threatening silences–okay?"

"Okay, Mary, I will do my best," he said in a somewhat shaky voice.

"We have to face up to the facts, John, this is the third chemotherapy and I still have metastasis in the liver and lymphatic system. I weigh forty six kilos and when I go to the toilet I bleed, my immune system is destroyed, I'm dying. When I die, you will be alone with two girls aged eleven and sixteen. Now I know that you have a lot of work to do and, because you have national and international responsibilities. There will be times when you will not be at home, so I am hoping that Consuela and Joan will help you. I have asked them both and they want to do all that they can to support you, Sarah and Caroline. All this is has been taken care of and I feel safe in saying that they are in good and loving hands. What I am worried about is you ..."

"You don't have to worry about me love, I can look after myself." he said, a little bit too fast and somewhat unconvincingly.

"Darling, I know that you can look after yourself. You know how to cook, you can drive a car, you know how to tie your tie–but that's not what I'm talking about." She stopped talking and took a deep breath. She looked out of the window where she could see the water shining silver out on the bay. She could see the golden beach of Bondi and could almost hear the people laughing and shouting, so free and happy. She continued: "John, do you remember all those years ago, when we were so young, travelling around Australia, enjoying each other

74

and enjoying life? Do you remember when we were at Coober Pedy on that very special evening looking out at the flat descrt so red and orange in the setting sun? There was this silence where you felt you could almost hear the earth breathing. We felt so near to each other and so near to each other's spirit. Do you remember what we talked about?"

John cleared his throat and said. "Yeah, I think we talked about how important it is to express our feelings and to be honest with each other even if it sometimes hurt. If I remember rightly we also talked about how important it is to respect each other and be willing to forgive if one of us did something harmful. Something like that, anyway."

"Well John, this is exactly where we are now. Over the last years, we have grown apart from one another. You make me feel guilty about taking on the partnership. We hardly speak with each other or to the girls. You have become almost a stranger. Yes, I feel hurt and angry and there are times when I want to punch you in the mouth, but then there are times when I feel like taking you into my arms and tell you that everything will be alright. Even now, in my fight against cancer, there were times when I really needed you, and you weren't there! Oh yes, in body perhaps, but not in the heart and spirit. Sometimes I felt resentment–even hate towards you–but there was always a little light in my head that said 'I love you' and this light never went out. At any rate, what I wanted to say to you is something that I learned in a dream last night." John swallowed back his tears as well as his impulse to interrupt her.

"I forgive you for hurting me, John. This does not mean that now all is forgotten and that I understand the reasons why you closed up your love to me. I still do not know why, but it doesn't matter anymore. All I want to do is to let go of the anger and the hardness that has been hanging around my heart for so long, so that you and I can once again show each other that we are in love."

"Darling, I don't know what to say, I feel so sad about letting it all get so hard and difficult. If only you hadn't taken on that partnership maybe things would have been different." Mary shouted: "That's exactly what I mean! You don't look at your part in this system. It's always me who's responsible and you are an innocent little bastard! Jesus, I'm so pissed off with you!" She lay back on her pillow fighting for breath. Her lips were turning blue and there were tears in her eyes. The alarm on one of the monitors was flashing red. John grabbed for the nurses bell and pressed down on the button. He shouted for help and just couldn't stop crying.

Fight to win
Fight for peace
Fight so that you....
Will never have to fight
again

Chapter 17

"**A**nd I haven't stopped crying inside since. I just haven't taken enough time to listen to what the tears have been trying to tell me. I blamed myself for your Mum dying like that, screaming at me, using her very last breath trying to teach me something about myself."

All three were silent, caught up in there own thoughts There were no answers in the air, no excuses or explanations it was just how it was and nobody could change it. The rest of the day was mainly filled with talking about the past, clearing up the misunderstandings that everybody felt. It was a very special day for the whole family: learning for the first time to be honest and open with each other; holding back nothing, except blame; and giving everything they had, to be able to walk closer to each other. Each knew, that this was just the beginning and, somehow, all three had the same feeling: that Mary was with them and the sun shone down on their little world the whole day .

He was lying in bed awake, thinking about the day together with his children He smiled, remembering the moment when Joan came sailing down to the water where they had been sitting. Looking around at the three of them, she said,

"Well all I can say is–it's about bloody time. Maybe now we can start to get on with really living instead of being stuck in the past and just talking about it. I just finished baking a plate full of lamingtons with whipped cream. Anybody interested?" We all laughed maybe a little bit too loud. It was almost as if the air around us wasn't yet quite used to hearing really happy voices. Then we stood up and walked together back to the house we called home.

Live with passion

Chapter 18

John closed his eyes. He found himself standing alone in the middle of the scrub, no shoes on his feet, naked except for a cloth tied around his middle. It was hot and still. He had a spear in one hand and a round flat stone in the other. He was standing perfectly still, waiting. He could see the goanna walking lazily up the track towards him, its head swaying from side to side, its blue-tinged forked tongue flashing in and out, tasting the air. He slowly raised the arm clutching the stone, holding his breath as if the world would stop turning, right at this moment. He aimed, without any doubt about missing, and launched the stone. It hit the lizard in the head and in the same instant as John threw the spear, it pierced the thick skin of the reptile's neck and, in an instant, it fell dead to the dusty ground. John walked up to the dead creature, kneeling down he put two fingers into the blood streaming from the neck of his prey and painted two stripes onto his forehead. He then muttered a small prayer of thanks to the soul of the lizard. He looked up and saw standing in front of him, the feathered man.

"Turawwa welcome back to the country!

"John shook his head as if to clear away cobwebs, and looking at the lizard he said. "What have I just done? I have never killed a living thing in my life, I consider

81

myself a pacifist and yet, I just killed a poor helpless lizard without blinking an eye."

The feathered man lifted the goanna from the ground by the tail; it must have been about three feet long. He looked at it and then at John: "This is your next lesson, Turawwa, to learn that souls that die keep the warrior alive so that he is able go on fighting for freedom and justice for the people he loves. A warrior knows no borders. You have already learned to trust your inner self, to believe in your own power, and to have the courage to express your feelings, but a warrior goes even further. Being connected to your past brings you the knowledge and dreams to create your life, just as now you were able to hunt and kill the goanna spirit even though you have never thrown a spear. A warrior lives in eternal peace, he knows no war, no battles, no hate, no fear, no discrimination, no anger, Yet he possesses the ultimate weapon–the power of passion!

When passion is ignited, it never stops burning, but it not only burns, it also brings light into the darkness and gives warmth where there is cold. You have turned off your passion in the past, because you were afraid of hurting others. This is your personal experience, but it is not the reality. In fact it is the direct opposite; when passion is not shown, you are not able to give of yourself and, through not giving, you are creating emptiness and pain within your loved ones. A warrior does not know the meaning of surrender.n At the moment when he recognises his vision, all his life force, feelings, thoughts and emotions are directed to achieving his goal and no power on earth can deter him.

However, the most strongest weapon that a warrior possesses is the power to love. You have learned a lot about love and, later in your quest, you will learn more about what love really is. But for now, it is only important to know that the love of life is the force that feeds you, the light that guides you and the army that fights at your side."

John heard a noise that sounded like thunder and in an instant the feathered man and the goanna disappeared. Once again, John was standing alone in a strange country.

"Hey, Turawwa, are you ready to learn how to throw the spear or do you want to rest in the sun and work on getting more brown?" John turned around and there was Wootara, standing beside a giant anthill, carrying two spears and a woomera under his arm.

"Wootara! Good to see you again, my boy!"

"I'm not your boy, I'm your teacher! So just shut your mouth and listen to your next lesson. A spear can only kill if it is thrown properly. Not only must your aim be true, but also your timing. Your eyesight is the direct line from you to your target. Your spear is the extension of your hand and the woomera is the extension of your arm. You must use your breath and count your heartbeats. So watch very, very, closely."

Wootara took the spear-launcher from under his arm. John could now see that it was shaped like a long oval with a small notch at one end and underneath a place where you could hold the woomera in your hand. He fitted one spear into the notch and let it lie straight on the surface, he then took hold of the grip, and drew back his arm, aiming at the tea tree standing about twenty yards away. Wootara took a deep breath, then with a loud exhale launched the spear. It left the woomera true and straight and struck the trunk of the tree, quivering in the hot air. "Throwing a spear is the same as wanting to make a point when you are speaking to your tribe. Your first step is to know your exact target and that which you want to be understood and then to hold this in your mind, in your heart and in your eyes. The next step is to be perfectly focused and still. Take a deep breath, count your heartbeats and breathe deeply. After you have counted ten heartbeats, let your spear fly and breathe your life-force out into the same direction as your spear,. Follow through with your body until you once again come to rest on both feet with your weight placed slightly more onto your right foot. A warrior expresses himself through the language of his body. That which he feels and that which he conveys through this body language must be in balance with his mind and spirit and fly true. Otherwise his spear will not be accepted by his partner, and the heart will not be pierced—and the heart is the place where you must always aim and never miss.

John understood perfectly what this boy was teaching him and couldn't help being impressed by the wisdom and clarity of the message. He walked up to where his little teacher was standing and took the other spear and the Woomera from his small scarred hands. He closed his eyes, forming an image of the tree inside his mind. Opening his eyes, he placed the end of the spear in the notch of the woomera, drew back his arm holding the spear-launcher and, without too much pressure, he aimed the tip of the spear at the tree, took a deep breath and on the tenth beat of his heart released the missile with a mighty cry. The spear landed three meters to the right of the tree and struck a rock. "Turawwa," said Wootara in an unusually polite tone. "Your aim was good, your breath and heart were perfectly in balance and your body danced the ways of the warrior. This time you did not pierce the heart, but with time and practice you will hit your target. You have learned how to throw the spear." Wootara's voice was becoming fainter and fainter and John noticed that the landscape was changing. Everything was starting to turn into a misty yellow and the last words that he heard were "...In the next dream the warriors path will continue ..."

John could smell the scent of fresh coffee wafting up the stairs coming from the kitchen. He sat up and once again as before, went through the memory of the dream, every image and every word. He even had a feeling that his shoulder felt sore caused by the unusual movements needed to throw spears.

*Prosperity without love is like a
tree without roots*

Chapter 19

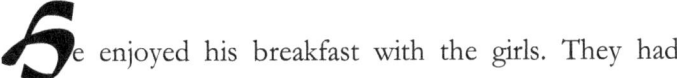e enjoyed his breakfast with the girls. They had asked him some more questions about the past, but strangely enough, he had the feeling that they wanted to know more about him and what kind of person he was, and less about how Mary passed away. Sadly, he also noticed that he had never before talked this way about himself with his children: openly, honestly, and to the point.

John walked out to the car and, for the first time in years did not feel like going to his office.

As he walked into the administration area, Mrs Simmons stood up from behind her desk and smiled. "Good morning sir. Before you start your agenda for today I would like to ...to ... give you something." She appeared very nervous and unsure of herself, something that John had never seen before during the years that they had been working together. She reached down into one of her immense drawers and took out a small cushion which was embroidered with a golden heart and, underneath, the words "Courage to lead."

"This is for you sir, I made it myself. Up until now, I never felt the need to give you a gift. But over the last few weeks, I've noticed the change in you. So, over the weekend, I had the urge to make this for you. I hope you like it." She pushed the small red cushion into his hands, sat down again and started tapping rapidly on her computer keyboard, her face almost as red as the cushion.

"Uhm ... thank you Mrs Simmons, it's very pretty and it will have place of pride in my study, so that everytime I look at it, I will think of you."

Mrs Simmons became even redder and John retreated into his office. He sat down and started taking notes, preparing himself for the meeting he had called together with all his aides, assistants and other people who worked for him inside Parliament House. He had a goal—the objective to clean up the whole administration structure—and he knew that there would be resistance and maybe even some aggression, but to be honest, he thought to himself,

"I'm just sick and tired of the dishonesty, intrigue and lack of unity inside of this system. I want to bring the heart into my way of running this country. Why can't we be more honest and open with each other? Why can't we talk about the problems and difficulties that we have and not just with the organisation, but also our own feelings of not doing enough—feelings of inadequacy and insecurity. Yes! Maybe even sometimes feelings of hopelessness. Feedback is the breakfast of champions! We need a spirit of working together, free of envy, jealousy, hate or misunderstandings. Yes! Of course this means more communication, more exchanges of ideas, but also creating the space and freedom where people can express and create new ideas and innovations to improve the quality of life on this continent."

John paused for a moment and took a few minutes to imagine what things would be like in the future if these ideals were implemented. He saw people becoming more self-reliant, creating new businesses and jobs for themselves. He saw the return of "micro-business" and shops where people could sell there ideas and products on a more human level, free of shopping complexes and multi-conglomerates. He saw the state of health improving, because people would start to healing themselves through complementary or natural medicine and the power of mind. He saw a hospital system run as a business where managers and workers could work hand in hand to create a place where healing was paramount and not illness. A place where normal medicine existed together with natural and eastern medicine. He saw a country full of windmills, solar energy projects and other energy producing centers that did not poison the atmosphere with carbon dioxide. He saw a land healing its rivers, beaches and forests so that nature once again could flourish in balance. He saw Aborigines and other minority groups working and living together with everyone else in a state of harmony. He saw a country full of people who were happy and proud to call themselves Australians.

John went into his change meeting feeling light and sure about his proposals he spent four hours talking and debating with his people. There was strong resistance and fear of change. But in the end, there was a feeling of hope and unity among his people. However, the price he paid was high. He had to let go of several members of his cabinet. Some of these people he used to call friends, but now they had become unhappy, angry ex-employees. John thought to himself; Three weeks ago I would never have thought that I would lead my people like this, it's like fighting a battle against an invisible army and the only way to win is through being consistent, without any compromise or half promises. It's an approach that goes against all the laws of diplomacy or political strategies, one that the girl with nine toes would most probably call hard love. He closed his office door and was looking forward to walking down to the river once again.

Friendship is a tree that gives
shade
when the sun is too strong
Food when we hunger
Strength when the wind becomes a
storm
And silence when confusion
reigns

Chapter 20

"*J*urawwa, now is the time to jump to the next stone. This is the stone of friendship." John was staring out at the water, listening to the girl's strange voice and wandering where she gets all this wisdom from. His concentration went back to what she was saying. "Friendship is a very special key that you need in order to be able to open doors to new worlds of experience. A friend at your side is like a mirror reflecting back what you do or say into your conscious way of thinking. Beware of a friend that's always paying you compliments, for that is exactly what he is doing–paying you to be nice back to him. A friend is the best critic you will ever find. He knows you inside out and has enough courage to tell you what he thinks. In some ways, a friendship is a more important realationship than a loving realationship between man and woman. There is no jealousy, no envy and no divorce proceedings if they separate. You are now standing at the junction of the track. Your way will now become more difficult. Many people will try to roll stones onto your path, some will even attempt to hurt you through negative thoughts, feelings and actions. Even though you must walk this path alone; you will need energy, support and minds that will guide you to success. This is the time to bring your friends together. Some of them have felt neglected in the past, during that time when you were closed up. But they are still there waiting patiently for you to invite them back into your future, all you have to do is to call them by name. Remember, Turawwa, friends are the water and nourishment that you need to be able to grow your vision tree. Without them the roots will become dry and neglected. Friendship is a two way track–giving and taking in balance. Where there are no demands or obligation, the spiritual tie is through the heart and that is what we call love. Where freedom, trust and believing in each other are the heart strings that create true friendship."

John looked at the small figure sitting on the rock, she was smiling and waved her hand to say goodbye. He turned up to the track leading onto the jogging path, thinking very deeply about what she had said. On one the one hand he felt very positive and hopeful; on the other, he felt unsure and in doubt. As soon as he got up to the path, he closed his eyes and searched for the place inside that was now his most important guide. Immediately, he felt more in balance and found himself putting more weight onto his right foot, on the side of his body that felt more secure, safe and positive."How did I know how to do that?" he said to himself. "She's probably using her brain waves again to manipulate me, that little beast!"

The two men on duty ran up to him, one of them said, "Sorry boss we lost you for about two minutes in the undergrowth, time to go home?" John nodded and followed his men in silence back to the car.

The world is a playground
So let's go out and play
Instead of going out to war

Chapter 21

 week later, John was sitting in his office thinking about all the things that had happened since he had last spoken to that girl. On Tuesday, he had organised a meeting together with Brian; John Catterall, Minister for Foreign Affairs; Peter Billingham, Minister for Industry, Tourism and Resources; and Geoff Brown, Minister for Education, Science and Training. He had known these men for many years and he could trust them with his life. They were men that he called friends.

"John," said Peter, "we don't really know what's been happening to you over the last few weeks; but, to be honest with you, we lost our trust in you, for a time. Over the years you have changed. You used to be like a bull in a china shop. Full of spit and guts—we respected you. You were sometimes doing your lone wolf thing, but at least we knew what your goals and visions were. Somewhere along the line—and I know I've said this many times over the past three years or so—either we lost you or you lost us."

The other men except for Brian nodded their heads as Peter spoke. Geoff was puffing on his German pipe. John was starring down at his hands. Brian was looking gruffly through his hooded, bushy eyebrows. "We've tried to steer this leaky boat through a recession, a small war and mounting unemployment rates. At times, we felt alone in our senate and state offices and even though our captain wasn't always standing on the bridge, I think we've done a fair job. John, we can see what you've been going through, Mary dying, you, losing your self confidence and all that trouble that you've had at home. But if we are going to stop this bloody boat from sinking, a lot of things will have to change. The memos that you're putting out and the unforgettable advisory meeting last week, as well as your speeches in parliament, remind me of the John I used to know. The changes you suggested are radical and for me, personally, I can also see you changing radically. I can't say exactly what it is, but I like it."

Brian smiled knowingly and sipped his tea.

"Jesus, John! Why can't you take that bloody cork out of yer' mouth and speak normally," laughed Geoff.

We've known each other for almost twenty years and your talking to John as if he's the prime minister of Australia and not our dearest friend." John turned a deep shade of red and closed his mouth.

"You've been a bastard over the last few years. You hardly ever talked to us. The only communication we have are through official communiqués. You looked like something the cat dragged in and your diplomatic prowess had been frozen on slowmo. John, I love and respect you and I can't say how happy I am to see that you've taken the ball into your own hands once again and that your're running instead of crawling. I also don't know what your're doing. Undergoing psychotherapy? Become enlightened? Or you've seen the holy ghost! All I know is that it's bloody great to be with you again, by the way, anybody for a beer?" He reached into his very large, old and battered briefcase and passed the bottles

96

around. Everybody laughed and cheered. John told his friends the whole story, Brian filled in on all the parts that he'd missed out. Everybody listened intently to the story, the only interuption was when the cook arrived from the canteen bringing in a large plate of fish and chips with tomato sauce and mayonaise that Brian had apparently pre-ordered. When John had finished telling them about what the girl had said about friendship they all just couldn't hold out any longer. "Cheers to friends!"shouted John and they all laughed together once again, clicking their bottles together. Even though all five friends felt light and cheery; inside their hearts, they all knew without a shadow of doubt that they had an ongoing battle coming up. A battle against the opposition, the cynics and old and new enemies.

"I can't tell you how thankfull I feel for your friendship and support. The four of you are like brothers. Brothers joined together to change this country. When I first met that girl, she said that I must learn to lead with the heart; now I have the feeling that you four are my heartstrings, leading my heart to beat the rhythm of a united Australia…"

"Jesus mate,cut it out will ya." said Geoff, "We're not here to hold ya' bloody hand and listen to your enlightened speeches about changing the world. We are here to fight together and whatever happens, I personally know that in a battle the best person to have on yar' side is a friend. And you've got four of these now sitting in your office drinking beer and putting tomato sauce stains onto your genuine merino wool carpet. So let's do what your girl down by the river said we should do and have some damn fun at the same time!" Everybody laughed and the sun went down behind Black Mountain marking the end of a very special day.

That evening after a great dinner with the girls, John went to bed early. As he closed his eyes, his thoughts went back to his four friends. He could hear their voices and almost smell there bodies as his mind drifted into another space in another time.

The past is the gateway to
changing the future

Chapter 22

*T*his time, the bush was much denser and all he could see were trees and thick banksia bushes with their deep red bottlebrush flowers and wattle trees which were fighting for the sunlight that was streaming weakly onto the forest floor. The light was somehow not quite there, but he could still see clearly all around in every direction. He could see the deep colours of the bush, madder red, amber and that red brown colour that sometimes almost turns to black. He could see patterns changing on the ground, depending on the light, turning into circles or curling snakes, always moving and turning, transforming the earth into a kaleidoscope of dancing forms, drawing him into their magic circle. He felt himself becoming hypnotised by the never ending patterns, changing and swirling on the ground, until the ground suddenly opened up and he fell into blackness.

He felt himself falling, deeper and deeper, his clothes flapping in the wind, he closed his eyes preparing himself to die and then, just as he started thinking about what Caroline and Sarah would do without him if he died he felt his descent slowing down-and then felt solid ground once again under his feet.

"John where have you been? I've been waiting for ages the film's about to start."

I gasped, hearing Mary`s voice, then I saw her standing under the red and blue lights of the "Civic Cinema", where we used to go when we first met, mainly to come together in secret and less to see the films.

"Sorry, darling, I got caught up in the traffic on Wentworth avenue, let's go get our tickets before it starts." We walked hand in hand to the ticket counter I paid for two tickets on the balcony. On the way, we stopped at the refreshments counter and bought a box of Toffifees and two Cokes. After finding our seats, I put my arm longingly around her shoulder. Smelling her perfume, I whispered into her ear, "Mary, I will love you forever." She whispered back.

"I will love you even longer."

The film was one of those arty french films about milky wood or something similar, but for Mary and me the film was not important, all that mattered was that we were together and not more than ten inches away from each other. As we walked back to the car, we talked about the daily happenings at the university, about my Mother who was planning on either murdering or divorcing my Father, and about the day on which we wanted to get married. The night was warm, it had just rained, and you could smell that familiar smell of wet asphalt as the steam rose off the road, giving the night that "Humphrey Bogart" feeling that Mary really loved. I could feel our bodies touching each other as we walked arm in arm to the car park.

"John where would you like to go for our honeymoon?" Her sultry voice pulled me out of my daydream back into reality.

"How about Coober Pedy?" I said, without even thinking.

"Yes, that's a great idea! Then you can show me the place where you grew up, the homestead, the school you went to. Coober Pedy's such a beautiful place-and full of opal shops!"

I smiled. "Okay my love, I'll start organising it, maybe we can stay in one of those underground hotels?"

"No fear mate!" she answered, shaking her head vigorously her long blond hair waving in the wind. "You forget that I get claustrophobia when I sleep in closed up spaces, how about a camper? My Dad knows a place where we can get a good price, then we can take our time driving up and stay wherever we want and...it's so romantic! And that's very important for a honeymoon or do you think otherwise? Mr John Raymond Macmilan."

I felt my face going red, looked down into her deep, blue eyes and mumbled in my best "Bogart" imitation. "Who am I to resist your irresistible womanly charms?" She looked back at me, then she took me into her arms and kissed me passionately standing in the middle of downtown civic center.

The next few weeks flew by very quickly, I received my bachelor of politics and commerce from the national university, Mary and I got married at All Saints church, my Mother filed for divorce, and we were ready to drive up to Coober Pedy in our rented, small but romantic camper. On the morning of our departure, we rose early. Looking out of the kitchen window I could see the sun coming up over Mount Ainslie and I knew it was going to be a fantastic day, full of sunshine and excitement ."John, have you packed the camera and film? What about the reserve water canister? And the new maps I bought last week, are they all in the glove box?"

"My darling, everything is packed and organised. Relax, put your feet, up and fasten your seat belt, South

Australia here we come!" I backed slowly out of the driveway, not yet used to the size of the vehicle, she put her hand on my thigh and, with the other hand, she opened up the road map.

"Relax? How can I relax with your sense of direction? I have to even give you driving directions when we go to Cotter dam for a day." she laughed.

When we got onto the highway, my mind started wandering, thinking back to the past, to the place where I lived my childhood. We owned a small homestead standing outside the opal fields. I remember the animals we had, the chickens, the sheep that I helped my father shear every spring, and our dog Frosty–a rather cantankerous Samoyed who never quite got used to swallowing dry yellow dust instead of freshly fallen snow. I remember the Aborigine camp, where a lot of my friends lived. The taste of my first witchity grubs, learning to throw a boomerang and play the didgeridoo.

But mostly I remember Waraala, dressed in feathers and painted with ochre mud, he taught me how to use the bull roarer and boomerang-the stories he used to tell us about the dreamtime and the earthy smell of his skin. We drove the whole day and towards evening when I started thinking again about my childhood Mary's voice brought me back to the present.

"John, turn right at the next exit, then keep driving for twenty five miles until we reach a bridge–maybe we can stop there by the river and take a rest."

"That's a good idea, my love. I'm starting to feel tired and we still have a good two hundred miles to go."

It was an old wooden bridge leaning over a small unknown river that was dry anyway. There were three weeping willow trees struggling to survive the heat on one side of the river, and on the other side there was a small flat area where we could park the camper."This looks great!" I said, looking up and down the dried up river bed. I could see nothing but sand and rocks and a few trees and bushes struggling for life, competing with the willow trees to survive. Mary walked up beside me and put her arm around my waist.

"Isn't it beautiful? So much space and freedom, unspoiled and pure-magical."

"Is that the lawyer speaking or the poet? But you are right, this is like standing at the beginning of time. This is the country untouched by human hands, unchanged, it almost seems like the earth was holding her breath to keep back time. I remember the colours and shapes at the time, where, as a boy, I would walk barefoot across our land. You could see people and animal forms in the rocks and ant hills, and, when the wind came up, you could almost hear the spirits singing. The older Aborigines used to talk about a very special spirit who could change lives, they used to call her the girl with nine toes. The old people used to say that she came whenever a great change was about to happen in the country and she always spoke with the elders–with the leaders of the tribes, teaching them how to make the right decisions by listening to their heart.,,

"That girl I would like to meet, but I would probably have to become the first female prime minister of Australia to attract her attention."

"Who knows what the future holds said the girl with nine toes." We both laughed aloud at my corny joke and the galahs sitting in the willow trees flew up to the steel blue sky.

We made ourselves a small fire and boiled up a billy full of tea. As the sun went down, we sat by the fire talking into the night. We stayed overnight beside that old dried up river and before I fell asleep I listened for a long time to the noises outside, the crickets chirping their relentless melodies, the rustle of the spinnafex rolling across the plain, driven by the hot, dry wind, and in the early morning light the laugh of a kookaburra waking us up to remind us about where we were bound. We hit the road at seven, in order to drive the last two hundred miles to our destination.

"John, tell me, why haven't you mentioned the story about the girl with nine toes before, you have talked about all those other dreamtime stories that you heard as a kid around the campfire with your aborigine friends, but never this one. Why's that?"

"No idea, love, it seems just to have escaped my mind and it popped up again in my memory recently. And anyway, it's one of those special ones that has it's own songlines and nobody seems to know what it really means. Waraala used to say that she could cross the bridge between reality and the dreamtime–that's like thinking with your conscious mind and your subconscious at the same time. Like setting up a dialogue, so that you can create your own future with what you know, what you knew, and what you will know in the next instant. Through this reality, you were able to change the future before it even happened. It all sounds rather complicated, maybe that's why I've put it in the back of my mind over all these years." I looked over at Mary and she had a really, weird look on her face, she smiled, "John do you know why I love you?"

"No darling, you tell me."

"Because whatever you do, and however often you try, you just can't hide behind your feelings, but the part of you that I love the most is your spirit. One day you will get to know this part of you and then you will know

105

that you are going home. John! Watch out, there's a snake on the road!"

I quickly steered in the other direction and soon had the van back under my control."Now why did that make me lose my concentration? This girl with the missing toe seems to be coming a part of our honeymoon, hope she's not moved into the back of the camper."

We soon arrived at the Coober Pedy camping site, turning into the driveway I could see the other campers and caravans, people all over the place, the souvenir shop. Everything was built for the comfort of the customers, even down to the "Opal Café", where you could sit under rainbow coloured sun umbrellas and drink tea or beer. I looked at Mary seeing in her expression exactly what I was thinking. I turned the camper around and drove back onto the road. "No way, Mary, I'm sorry I didn't realise that it had become so modern. I remember a more natural camping site with trees and bushes instead of plastic and beer tables and there used to be a little creek at the back that sometimes even had water in it." Mary simply laughed.

"Ah! John, don't worry about it, let's just drive out into the bush, maybe near where you lived. There should be some place where we can make camp and if we need to get some water or load up the battery then we'll just drive into town."

It had been fifteen years since I had left for Canberra, but it felt like fifteen days. The roads were the same, the shops and pubs and the opal seller's shops were the same, the only thing that seemed to have changed was the camping site. As I drove down the main road, I felt somehow as if I was coming home, and at the same time had the feeling of being a stranger in a strange land. It was almost as if I had left something here and had to come back and take it away with me to complete a circle-something that would help me in the future. Soon we came to a large, flat, plain stretching out to the horizon, dotted here and there with those typical conical hills of the opal mines. I turned off the motor and all we could hear was silence, a perfect silence—deep and profound. The silence of Kupa Piti, the aboriginal name meaning white man in a hole. "This takes my breath away, I can vaguely remember how quiet it was here, nothing distracts you from your thinking. It's like the bush is teaching you to go inside and listen, do you know what I mean?"

"What .... what did you say, darling? Sorry, I was just so deeply taken away by the landscape and the beauty that I didn't hear everything you said. It's amazing, look how the land touches the sky at the horizon, red on red, I can't tell where the land ends and the sky begins. I can smell the dust and something else, that smells almost like Sage. This silence is like being inside an immense cathedral, a spirit place, yes that's what I'd call it-The place of the spirits."

We climbed out of the camper and started looking around for wood to make a fire. Everything was so dry and still warm to the touch, even though the sun was melting into the earth on an unbroken line thousands of miles away. We soon had a good fire going; and sitting on a blanket, we looked towards the sunset, watching the orange, red and yellow curtains of fading light fall down to the burning soil.

"You know when we sit here, I can't help thinking about the past, it's not all quite clear in my mind, there were so many influences from so many different sides. On one side, I was working on the farm together with my father and brothers, my father was very strict and our daily lives were full of rules, duties and responsibilities, and on the other side, the old people and Waraala, sitting down on the warm earth listening to his voice and the stories and legends of the dreamtime–the songlines, and not forgetting the girl with nine toes. You remember how I told you that when I was twelve I almost died of an infectious heart disease and how Waraala came to our house feeding me obnoxious teas and leading me into trance states to meet the spirit healers? And then, after three weeks, I opened my eyes to a new day, where the sun was shining and I wasn't burning with fever. All these memories are somehow confusing, flowing into each other like a tapestry of the past, woven together with threads of reality and of imagination. I can see the whole picture, but there are a lot of holes where I sometimes go swimming. It's like becoming a part of the earth-I feel this strong connection to a power that I can't describe, and yet a power that lends me strength and clarity, teaching me to trust my emotions and my intuition, to believe in myself and the love within my heart. But somehow, being in Canberra has drawn me away from this state of being. Now I seldom go swimming within the songlines, and my everyday life is filled with lectures, exams and reality. Then I notice how I change, I become restless and lazy and start feeling guilty, or start blaming, rationalising everything with my brain instead of my heart. Coming back here has reminded me about my home and where my roots are. Being here with you is like introducing you to my other parents, to the place where I grew up. I'm just wondering if you also love this place as much as I do–whether or not you also feel the connection–and simultaneously afraid that you might think that I'm crazy or suffering from sunstroke."

"No John, I know what this place means to you. This is your place of birth and I feel that you learned much wisdom and knowledge here. I understand some of what you say and the rest is like ...like looking into a mirror trying to find out what's behind the glass–I can see the reflections, but I am still standing outside. And about you being crazy? I know you are–that's why I love you so much." She smiled her magic smile and I threw another piece of wood onto the fire. "I also sense a kind of power radiating from the earth. Something like vibrations that you can feel in the air, but you know me, I react from the mind, I have to actually hold something in my hand before I can say that I know what it is. I'm a realist and you're a dreamer, but that's probably why we get on so well with each other." She leaned her head onto my shoulder and I could smell the smoke mingled with the scent of shampoo in her hair. We kept talking, watching the red sun disappear, talking about our realationship, about love and expressing our emotions even if it could hurt each other, to be open and honest with each other. Soon we were sitting in silence, enjoying each other in the stillness. I was looking through the fire and could see what looked like white dust gathering up into a form that appeared to be almost human, a man, sitting cross legged arms akimbo. A voice floated through the flames ."Welcome home, John it has been a long time since these old and tired eyes saw you last."

"Waraala!" I shouted, looking quickly in Mary's direction to make sure she hadn't fainted. I went over to my old friend, I hugged him carefully and felt his frail, pointy bones sticking through the baggy shirt he was wearing, he patted me lightly on the back.

"John, my son, I am hear for a reason. There is something that I must teach you, it is something that you will forget in the future, but it will come back to you like the boomerang, at that time in your life when you stand at the crossroads of failure or success." He called Mary over to sit next to him.

"You, my daughter are also a part of this tapestry, without you we would have no thread and with no thread we would not know in which direction to weave our story. We knew that you were coming back today and we have waited for many years to give you what I will give you tonight. A man is born with three parts, the body, the heart, and the spirit. The body moves him through the world and protects and nourishes him. The spirit guides him to the Lizard and Snake man in the sky and the earth , and the heart teaches him to live in love. Love means to have the courage to show all feelings and emotions wherever you are and whoever is with you. The old ways have been, by many forgotten, but, when you were a boy, I saw that your heart was very strong and the song within your heartstrings told of your future. It is not allowed that I tell you exactly what will happen in your life in the future, my task is only to give you one helping hand to show you which direction to take. I am your past, and the past reflects into the future. Walking our life path we may come to situations and crises where we fail to see the sun. Instead we tend to bask in the shadows of despair and failure. Standing in the dark you cannot see the path back into the sun, here you have to turn around and look back at where your footsteps have led you to. In your future, both of you will meet the girl with nine toes and she will be your guide, listen to her and you will change, just as the colours of the giant rock change from dawn to sunset. John, this is the gift that the circle of the wise men asked me to give you." He reached into the dilly bag hanging over his shoulder and pulled out a white feather. "This is

110

the feather that connects you to your home. It used to belong to a spirit man who, a long time ago, led his people into peace, teaching them how to live a life where an open heart opened doors. This feather will open the doors that you will need to walk through, into the future." He laid the feather in my hand and lifted his arms up towards the fading light.

A wind blew across the desert turning everything into dust. I felt my body slowly turning around and around in circles, I had a sensation of being lifted up, off the warm earth and. As I opened my eyes, I could see the weak sun shining through my bedroom window. I opened my hand and saw a white feather fluttering in the breeze that was whispering through the open window. I closed my hand around it and laid it down in the top drawer of my dresser knowing that some day soon I would be needing it.

*Follow your dreams and they
will follow you*

Chapter 23

"Mr Prime minister, you cannot be serious, this is a joke. How can you possibly believe that our indigenous population can survive if we don't provide shelters, homes and places for them where they can live in houses like every other human being? Now you are saying that you want to give them back their land so that they can live as they had lived in the past. Not only that, you also want to give them money, so that they can start there own businesses make and sell their spears and boomerangs and give didgeridoo lessons. Up till now you have been quite happy with the aid programmes for Aborigines, keeping them safe and controlled. Now you want to set them free!"

"Mr Norton, we cannot turn the indigenous race of this country, free because they are not prisoners or slaves. They are a free people just like you and me, and I feel that it is high time that this government treated them as such. We have been playing the role of the colonizer for over two hundred and fifty years–these people do not feel free. We demand that they assimilate into our culture, live in houses, drive cars and work for money. Some of the new generation do just that, they even attend universities and do, take their rightful place in the community. But I'm talking about another situation.

About the people, who can't cope and simply just do not understand our way of living. Those who become alcoholics, unemployed and desperate–and why? I will tell you why, Mr Norton, these human beings have lost their homes, their heritage and their spirit. I say, let's give the indigenous people of Australia back their land where they can once again be what they truly are–Australians.!"

He went back to his seat, feeling the angry glare not only of Mr Norton, but also of others in the hall. He also could see the shining eyes of his supporters and his friends, and this gave him strength.

"Ladies and gentlemen of this government. I and every member of my party support Mr Prime Minister in his vision of racial equality. We also believe that it is high time for this country to have the courage to take radical steps towards change, even if some among us still live in fear of being invaded my a black holocaust of spear throwing heathens."

"Mr Billingham, if that statement is referring to me, then I ask you to cease your provocations or there will be consequences!" shouted Mr Norton.

My friend Peter continued.

"Whatever you want to believe, Mr Norton, the map is not the territory. We are not fighting against you, we are not trying to defame you. We are merely trying to lift this country onto a higher plane of integrity, where truth and the courage to be different are everyday qualities of life, instead of a rarity!" Geoff, Brian and John stood up in unison clapping there hands and, smiling, many other members of parliament also stood up and applauded. I looked up at the wall where that painting was hanging and thought I could see a trace of a smile on that grim face of the lone aborigine holding his spear.

Decide to live
Not suffer

Chapter 24

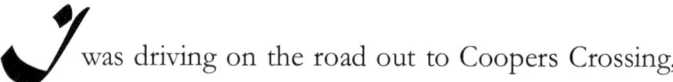was driving on the road out to Coopers Crossing, once again enjoying my freedom, without having my two shadows following me. I could see a small white delivery van behind me, which was flashing its headlights, trying to overtake me. I braked, the van drove by, then all of a sudden it steered into my path. I braked hard and came to a standstill I could smell burning rubber. Two men wearing ski masks jumped out of the van. I reached into the glove box to get out my revolver, but I was too late. They ripped the door open, dragged me out of the car and pulled me over to where the van was standing with the motor running. I could see a third man sitting behind the steering wheel. Throwing open the rear door, one man pushed me into the back of the van and put a cloth over my mouth and nose. I struggled and could smell that almond, pungent scent of chloroform, the world turned black.

I could hear what sounded like the noise of a small plane in flight, my head felt terrible and I wanted to be sick-but I took some deep breaths and tried to relax and get myself oriented. My eyes were bound up tight, I couldn't see a thing. It was hot inside the plane and I could sense one or two other people sitting beside me. "Mr Macmilan can ya' hear me?" said a deep, rough voice.

"Yes I can, where are we? What do you want ? Do you want money? How much?"

"Just keep ya' mouth shut mate, an everythin' will be alright"

I felt my sense of reality fading again, I closed my eyes and slipped once again into that cool, black world of unconsciousness.

We must have landed, because I could hear the sound of the plane's motor getting slower and slower, eventually the plane stopped and I felt two strong hands gripping my arms, pulling me out of my seat onto the dusty ground.

The deep, rough voice said. "Keep on walkin' till I tell you to stop."

I could smell the dust of the outback and the sun burning relentlessly down onto my head and neck, I still felt groggy and weak, but by taking deep breaths and concentrating on that place of balance within, I started to take stock of my situation. My hands were tied tight behind my back. I couldn't feel my fingers. I was blindfolded and had no idea where we were. I was outnumbered by at least three to one. I had left my mobile telephone in the car and I was an absolute bloody fool for going out without my bodyguards.

"Climb up into the jeep mate! It wont be long now, and you'll get a beer and some tucker!" His laugh reminded me of a hyena with hiccoughs. It took about half an hour to get to our destination. The jeep braked, I was once again dragged across the ground into what felt like a house. It smelt of stale sweat and beer. I heard a door being opened and I was then pushed into a room. Somebody untied my hands and I felt pain and an unbearable tingling sensation in both of my arms. The blindfold was ripped off my head and I blinked my tear-filled eyes trying to see into the blinding light. I heard footsteps behind my back and the sound of a door closing; I was being being locked in from the outside. After a few minutes my eyesight started coming back and I could make out shapes within the room: a bed, two chairs and a small table under a window that was boarded up with plywood. I sat down on the bed and once again went inside to that place where I could hear the spirit voices. I felt a sensation of calmness and strength slowly spreading throughout my body. I placed my hand on my chest at that place, where I knew from my talks with the girl unconsciously triggered a state of clarity and inner strength. Somehow, I knew that the men who kidnapped me did not want me to stay alive for a very long time. Looking around the room again, I noticed a small cassette player on the table under the boarded up window there was a piece of paper lying beside it that said: "play me" I pressed the play button.

"Good evening Mr MacMilan." The voice was slow and high pitched "Welcome to my hideway out in the country. Now you might be asking yourself what do these people want from you? I can assure you that it is not money. We are part of a society whose aim it is to keep Australia pure and clean—we believe in the pureblood Australian. We have noticed that you have started new reforms for the Blacks and you, especially, should know how dangerous these animals are to our white community.**

We have tried and judged you—and find you guilty of treason against our fair country. Your sentence is the penalty of death. You may have sensed coming in that we are deep in the outback. In

118

fact the next living person lives over two hundred miles away. This is the desert, Mr Prime Minister. Outside the temperature ranges from thirty–forty five degrees. There is nothing but sand, rocks and death. Quite soon, one of my friends will come and take you for a short drive. He will bring you to a very special place and leave you there alone. There is absolutely no possibility that you will survive more than twenty four hours–even your black friends have left this part of the country. Mr Macmilan, I want to take this opportunity to wish you an uplifting walk in the valley of death where you will no doubt die!" The recording ended and immediately the door opened. Two of the men came into the room and pulled me off the chair. I was once again blindfolded as they took me outside to the jeep and strapped me into the seat. The man with the hyena laugh whispered into my ear: "Go to hell, you bastard!" His breath smelled like garlic and stale beer and I was more than glad when the jeep started up and drove away. The track was first of all very rough and bumpy but after a while, I got the feeling that we were driving over smooth sand. It seemed like a very long time before the jeep stopped, I was pulled roughly out of my seat and thrown onto the ground. As they drove away, I could hear the hyena laughing between his hiccoughs. I ripped off the bag that they'd put over my head and opening my eyes; I experienced a deep and desperate sensation of shock. I could see nothing but sand and rocks reaching out far into the horizon. I turned around in a circle and nothing changed. Looking down at my shoes I noticed that I was still wearing my office shoes. I knew that they would keep out the heat for a while, but how long would they last?

Turawwa follow the spirit lines they will show you the way. Well, at least my inner voices are still working, I thought, as I started walking through the blazing heat. As I walked, I started thinking back to the past, remembering the faces of Waraala, Mary, the girl with nine toes, my daughters and my friends. I was now on automatic pilot, trusting my intuition and the spirit lines, but I became very tired in a very short time. I could feel the saliva drying up in my mouth. I put a small pebble into my mouth and started sucking on it, knowing that this would stimulate the flow of saliva, but I did not know for how long. I noticed the sky becoming a deeper shade of blue and my shadow was getting longer-I had to find water soon. Looking ahead, I focused on finding a place where the ground appeared deeper, remembering the old way of finding water. I was searching for a depression in the sand where I knew, if I could dig deep enough; and if I was lucky, I would find water. Some way ahead, I could see some stunted mulga scrub—this was sometimes a sign telling where water could be found. It felt like hours until I reached the small clump of bushes, but I could see a small gully in front of the scrub throwing shadows where it seemed to get deeper. I broke off one of the branches of the nearest tree and started digging at the deepest part of the small gully, the perspiration poured down off my body and I felt dizzy with exhaustion, but I kept on digging. I dug down to the depth of about one meter when I noticed the sand becoming darker and moist. I croaked, with joy, as loud as I could, when I saw a small puddle of water forming at the bottom of the hole. The water was dirty and tasted salty and stale but I felt my tongue and throat greedily sucking in the moisture so that my body recovered some of its energy. I lay down under the meagre shade of the mulga scrub and closed my eyes.

When I woke up, I was startled and didn't know where I was. Everything was as black as night and I felt cold and hungry. I reached down into the hole and drunk a few hand fulls of water; I felt better.

I was Looking down at the roots of the mulga scrub and remembered that honey ants sometimes build their nests beneath the roots of mulga. I started digging frantically, I hadn't eaten for at least twenty four hours, and then I found them, big black ants with their amber coloured pouches glued to the rear of their bodies. I found a twig; I turned over one of the ants and picked it up between two fingers and bit of the honey filled sac: it tasted wonderful. I hadn't tasted anything as wonderful in my whole life; with all the digestive juices inside my mouth my tongue sizzled on overload. I ate about ten of the honey globules and I felt much better. I was now confronted with the problem of how to carry the water. I knew that I had to keep going and that during the night was the best time to walk, avoiding the energy sapping heat of the sun. I took off my shirt and soaked it in the waterhole. Putting it back on I thought that I would at least have some moisture on my skin for the next few hours. I started dog-trotting, walking quickly for a few minutes then slowly for the same length of time. The time was difficult to judge as my watch had been taken away when I was unconscious. The sky was filling with diamonds, I could see the Southern Cross and, judging by the stars, I was going in a south easterly direction. Sometimes I would stop still, asking myself if the direction I was going was still right. I wished that Bongo was here to help me decide. I noticed the vegetation was also slowly changing, there was less sand and there were more stones on the ground. I also noticed that my feet were hurting like hell, I was feeling thirsty and hungry again, and my shirt was as dry as a bone. I could see the horizon slowly becoming lighter-a yellow orange haze was forming on the sharp ridge of rocks that I could just see in the distance. My second day in the desert was beginning and I needed to find some shade, and that ridge of rocks looked just like the right place. When I arrived at the rocks, the sun had risen, I could see steam rising from the stones, drying off the early morning dew. Straight away I bent down, feeling under the edge of the largest rock. I was looking for a hole that might lead me to Tiddalik the water holding frog. Waraala used to tell us children that these frogs could save our lives. When it rained in the desert, they soaked up a tremendous amount of water in and around their skin; then they burrowed themselves into the sand, under rocks to wait for the next rains. Yes! There it was–a hole under a large stone. I started digging with my hands and, even though they were scratched and bleeding, I did not stop until I felt the slimy cool mass. I closed both my hands around the large frog and slowly lifted him out of the hole. He was brown and red in colour; his eyes were closed he felt heavy in my hands. I tried to remember what Waraala said about these givers of life, and then I remembered. I held him above my mouth and squeezed his body gently, the pouch of water around his body broke and the sweet, clear water flowed into my mouth. I let the rest of the water flow onto my shirt, wrapped it up tight and pushed it under the rocks where it was cool and shady. I let the frog crawl back into the sand, thanking God that he had created this wonderful, ugly looking saviour. I was hungry and I knew that I needed to eat to keep up my strength. Tiddalik was not edible so I started searching around the rocks and under the spinnafex grass for something to eat. Except for dried out beetle husks and seeds, I found nothing. All of a sudden I started to cry, letting out all the anger and frustration that I had been holding in, up till now. I was even pissed off with all the spirits and the girl with nine toes. Where were they all now? I asked myself. Where were the miracles and magical dreamtime stories that could transport me instantly back to Canberra and safety? I cried until all my tears dried up beneath the relentless sun, then I curled up into a ball under the shade of the rocks and spinnafex grass and went to sleep.

Waking up I thought that I had died. I felt exhausted and dried out. I could not feel my hands or my feet and my head felt like it was going to explode. The first thing that I did was pull my shirt out from under the rock and it was still moist with water. I started sucking on the cloth feeling my life energy slowly returning. It was early evening and looking around I saw something green behind a large clump of spinnafex. I walked over and saw that it was an Emu Bush. I cried out with relief ande grabbed a handful of the leaves I saw the yellow succulent bodies of the emu bush grub clinging to the underside of the scimitar shaped leaves. I ate ten of them, trying to imagine that they were sushi, but my imagination wasn't working up to scratch and they only tasted oily and bitter. But I knew that they contained lots of protein, so I swallowed them down. Soon the diamonds began to twinkle in the blue, black, velvet sky once again, I started walking. My legs and feet were aching and even though I had rubbed some of the healing sap of the emu bush into my hands they were swollen and red. I kept walking, still knowing when to turn and when to go straight ahead. Otherwise, I had lost all contact to my inner spirit songs, all I could hear was the scuffing sound of my shoes as they carried my body wearily across the desert floor. I had been walking for a

123

very long time, there was no more moisture to suck from my shirt–my mouth was dry and blistered and all I wanted to do was to sit down and go to sleep. I felt an almost overwhelming, inviting desire to surrender to my fate and then I remembered those first words she had said "Do you want to live or die?"

"I want to live!" I whispered hoarsely to myself, "I want to live!"

I closed my eyes and walked.

I closed my eyes and listened.

I closed my eyes and felt.

I closed my eyes and lived.

I felt my body being lifted up by somebody, and opening my eyes I could see Baldwa's face looking into my eyes. He said. "Your pain will flow along the rivers of time to the place where memories are nothing but footsteps in the sand on a peaceful beach."

*If that what you do, does not work,
Then do something else*

Chapter 25

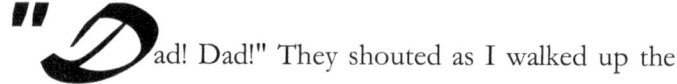

"ad! Dad!" They shouted as I walked up the steps to the house, Sarah crying with all her heart and Caroline doing all she could not to cry, but not quite succeeding. I hugged them both tight and we only let each other go when Joan complained that if we did not shut the door, the house would be full of blood-sucking reporters inside five minutes.

"Its good to be home." I said

"Dad we were so happy to hear your voice when you phoned yesterday! We thought ... we thought ...that we would never see you again."

"Joan's been driving us nuts doing tarot cards every five minutes and screaming blue murder everytime she turns over the hanged man card."

"Uncle Brian and Auntie Connie came over yesterday. I think I saw uncle Brian crying when you rung up, but I bet he'll deny it and say something like, 'Big boys don't cry!'"

I bathed in their joy and passion. I felt so relieved to see their shining eyes and hear their angel voices. The bell rang, and I heard Joan giggling like a schoolgirl and I knew that it couldn't be anyone but Brian. I looked up to see not only Brian, but also John, Peter and Geoff. Geoff carried a case of Fosters under his arm and Brian carried a smile on his face that could have made the sun shine in the middle of a hurricane.

"Hey, you stupid bugger, getting lost in the desert!" shouted Peter, putting his arms around me.

"I knew all the time that you'd make it back!"said John.

"Yeah, he even laid down some bets with his advisors and won a small fortune!"

"You and your big mouth Geoff, but if I remember rightly, did not I see you putting a ten dollar bill into your wallet that Ray MacNamara had put into your hand, as you both were standing outside in the car park this mornin' ?"

Brian came over and almost broke my ribs giving me a bear hug, then he punched me in the arm and said "Good to see ya' again mate, I've been scared stiff the last three days."

John pulled us apart and gave me a sloppy kiss on the cheek and said absolutely nothing–which I thought very unusual.

They all sat around the table opening up bottles of beer, while Joan hurried over to bring glasses that nobody noticed. Caroline and Sarah excused themselves and hurried away upstairs.

"Did John tell you that we found the bastards?" asked Brian.

"One of the Aborigines that found you—I think his name was Baldy or something like that–put two rangers onto the right track leading up to the place where they were holding you. It was raided six hours ago. They found all kinds of right-wing propaganda, weapons and artillery , as well as five men who won't be out of jail until their hearts stop beating." We all cheered,and then I started to tell my dearest friends how I survived those three days in the desert, getting interrupted every now and again by Brian telling jokes about bush grub, Frogs that could bite your toes off and other attempts at hiding his feelings. John told us that the statistics state that the survival time in that part of the desert was between six to twelve hours. I knew that I was lucky but I also knew that, if I hadn't heard those stories many years ago and if I had not met that girl with nine toes, then I would surely have perished out there beneath a merciless sun. I soon started feeling really exhausted even though the Flying Doctors had given me an infusion and something for the pain in my hands and feet. I knew that I would need a few days to get my strength back. I walked my friends to the front door and I watched them walk over to their cars. I came back into the house. Joan called me into the kitchen, where she had made some fresh lamingtons. Sarah and Caroline were already there, filling there mouths with coconut and chocolate covered cake. Caroline swallowed down her cake, stood up, and coming over to me slapped me solidly in the face. "I want you to promise me right here and now that you will never, ever go anywhere without your bodyguards. Swear on your life right now."

My cheek was burning and my eyes filled with frog water. I could see her eyes glistening and her lips quivering. Sarah was standing behind her with her hands on her hips staring at me the same way Mary used to when she was angry. I responded, "I swear on my life that I will never go anywhere without my bodyguards, but only if you swear never to sleep with a boy without using a condom." They both screamed and hugged me at the same time. Then we all three broke down and cried our hearts out and Joan shacking her head put the kettle on for a fresh cup of tea.

The heart feels
The mind thinks
And the body follows

Chapter 26

I could hear Bongo barking and smelled the smoke before I could see the people sitting down around the campfire. Watoora came running up to me and threw his arms around my legs and Bongo nipped playfully at my ankles. I walked into the circle and they were all there, Waraala, Baldwa the Feathered One and the other faces that I remembered seeing last time I was here. I sat down and the same old lady came over to me and gave me a mug of bush coffee–she smiled at me through her toothless gums.

The Feathered One spoke. "Turawwa, this is the last time that you will sit in this circle. We have guided you through challenges that will change your life. You have learned to trust yourself and to believe in your intuition. You have learned to see the spirit within people to know who is with you and who is against you. You have learned about love. You have learned how to throw the spear of clarity teaching you to speak with your heart. You have learned about the strongest love between people, friendship. You have found once again your courage that you once lost. You now know how to make your vision become a reality.

In the past, you were locked within the walls of self pity and the addiction to suffering. Your ears were closed to the words of your loved ones and your spirit turned to the moon instead of the sun. We did not help you when you walked through the Fire snake desert, because we knew that you must survive using your own wisdom and knowledge—alone. Now that you have started walking on the path of the leader that leads with the heart, you will never stand still and, moving forward, the songlines will change just as you have changed. The true warrior knows only love and passion and these two brothers will walk at your side as of today and will never leave you. My last lesson for you, my son, is mirrored in my dress, I am the feathered one, and a feather is so light that it can even fly. But even when it floats on the winds of the past, it will always return to the earth that exists only in the time of now. The feather will heal you of your guilt so that you can enjoy a life of lightness and fly in innocence."

I could see the wrinkles around his eyes getting deeper as he smiled a crooked smile. Then he came up to me, took both my hands into his gnarled sandpaper-dry hands, and surrounded in utter silence turned into smoke. Looking around at the others, I could see them all waving their hands to say goodbye. Then the smoke of the fire swept over the meeting place and my friends returned one by one back to the dreamtime. I sat down on the empty ground and opening my right hand I saw the white feather lying there, fluttering in the breeze. I closed my eyes and going deep inside I could hear her voice calling me.

"John? My love are you now ready to listen?" I opened my eyes and I could just make out what looked like her face in the flames of the fire.

"We have been allowed to speak with each other, but just this one time my darling. This is a time for forgiving. A part of my soul still feels the hurt caused by your words, but at the same time I know that you have paid the price over the years. My heart lives on within the heart of our two daughters, as well as the memory of you. Remember me as the person who loved you more than anything else in the world. Life must go on, knowing that behind every tragedy there is a message to understand. And my message to you is the reality that giving for love means taking for love and when two independent hearts are open for each other then love will live forever and when they are not open, a part of this love will die. Listen to the girl with nine toes!" The fire went out and I sat alone filled with the voice of Mary and her words turned to ashes.

Stand up, stand up
And show your face to the
sun
Wake up, wake up
And open your eyes to the
truth
That the truth is you

Chapter 27

I walked over to the dresser and opened the drawer, I saw that the feather was gone. I walked out of my bedroom, along the corridor to the kitchen smelling the coffee and yesterday's lamingtons, and went out the back door. When I got outside onto the grass, I took off my shoes and walked down to the water. I needed time to think and get myself sorted. The intensity of last night's dream was still lingering within my body. Looking down at my hands I suddenly realised that all the blisters and sores had disappeared. The work of those old gnarled sand paper-dry hands I guess. I had a feeling deep inside that I would not see my friends of the dreamtime ever again. Friends that had changed my life and guided me back to that what I really am. Faces. Smiles. Voices. Smells. Words and Visions that showed me which path to take. Whispers within the night of the past. Butterfly wings touching my soul. The smoke of knowledge blowing in the winds of reality. Filling my sails with hope, trust and joy.

But above all the most passionate gift of all, Love without guilt, love without fear, love without anger. I will never forget you.

When you have reached a goal
begin a new one

Chapter 28

Twelve Months later:

*W*alking into my office, I was feeling lighter and stronger than I had ever felt in my life. The colours and shades of light were so intense and in focus that I had a feeling as if I were living in a new world.

Mrs Simmons reminded me of a slightly overweight Greta Garbo as she looked up at me, smiled and chirped: "Good morning, Mr Prime minister!"

I opened the door to my office to see my four friends and a surprise guest, Mr Norton, accompanied by his personal assistant Stephen Fortescue, all seated in front of my desk. They all stood up and clapped their hands as I edged around to my seat, I sat down feeling a little bit embarrassed.

Brian started "John, I am proud and moved to present to you the results and goals achieved by our government since you personally instigated the reformation process. Because of a changing consciousness in self-responsibility within the citizens of Australia, our economic debt has decreased by thirty five percent. Over fifty two percent of the population is now self-employed. Fifty five percent are women. The unemployment rate has sunk to three point two percent and is sinking continually. Over ninety percent of all Australian products are now made on our own soil instead of using cheap labour in poorer countries. The people of our country are learning, slowly but surely, what it means to achieve prosperity awareness. People are even organising credit card burning demonstrations, to show that they no longer wish to live a life weighed down with financial debt and the fear of not having enough money. Almost everybody pays cash when they buy products and the credit card companies have been transformed to 'Coaching for Prosperity' companies teaching people how to earn and manage their own finances. Gentlemen, this country has changed from a country on the verge of national poverty into a land of prosperity, where almost everybody believes that he has more than enough instead of never enough."

I squirmed uncomfortably in my seat, taking the folder that Brian presented to me over my desk. We shook hands and I could almost read his mind searching for some sort of suitable joke but, for once, he was silent and I could see his eyes shining.

"Thank you Brian, and John what about you?"

"Well our foreign policy reform is in full swing, John. Our partnerships with third world countries have been doubled. Because of our "Use Your Own Hands"-projects, in which we teach the people of poor countries how to build and purify there own water resources, farm their land and organise fair trade agricultural organisations, the quality of life has risen. Together with local governments, we have also built up branches of The Flying Doctor Service, which enable medical support teams to go into isolated regions to treat malaria, leprosy and AIDS. As well as this we have trained teams of medical assistants to work as "Barefoot doctors" in all areas where poverty and malnutrition reign. We still have much to do but we are winning. As well as this, our relationships to Middle Eastern countries has intensified, especially since you introduced the Australian Muslim integration programme. We are working hand in hand together with Europe and America on international standards for protecting and healing the world of global pollution. All in all, I would say we are making lots of friends!" He smiled at me and winked, as he put his coffee stained folder into my hands.

"Okay Peter, how's it with you?"

"You know me John I don't like talking too much so I will be short and go straight to the point. Industrial production has increased by thirty percent! At the same time, because of the use of alternative energy programmes, emission rates have fallen by forty percent. Your Green Tourist Programme, encouraging people from other countries to experience the outback, the Queensland rain forests, and other protected areas that exist in harmony with nature, to learn how to be ecologically aware, is booming. We have discovered new sources of natural gas in South Australia and Tasmania and, therefore, our need for fossil fuel has fallen thirty percent. The rest is in here."

He handed me such a thick folder I had to take it with two hands, it was very heavy.

"Thanks, John!" Geoff was next.

"Well, John, a lot has changed over the last twelve months in the area of education. We have finally realised that children are human beings and not sheep. We have taken down all the bricks in the wall and are now building schools without walls. Schools where children and young people can learn in an atmosphere of support and understanding instead of fear and pressure. Since you created the "Teacher–Teach Yourself" Programme, which trains teachers to understand their own hidden negative belief systems and develop personal clarity, especially in the field of communication, schools and universities have become gardens of learning. Aggression and drug abuse has decreased by sixty five percent. Children now feel safe and secure when they go to school. Our science and innovation reform has skyrocketed into unbelievable realms of new ideas and discoveries, thanks to the new research centers that are open for anybody who has a good idea. All I can say is, it's bloody incredible!" He gave me his folder and punched me playfully on the chin.

Then, James Norton stood up.

"Sir, I am not one of your personal friends, at least not yet! But I would like to take this opportunity to thank you personally for what you have done over the last twelve months. Australia has changed her course radically! I want to congratulate you on what you have been doing to improve the rights and life qualities of the people in this country, especially those of the Aborigines. I admit that I was very sceptical about the sudden changes that you brought forward, and was also very wary about your personal changes. I even entertained the idea that you were using mood enhancing drugs, marijuana or even Scientology. I even heard some vague rumour about a new girlfriend who lives near the Murrumbidgee river. Anyway, to cut a long story short, Mr Macmilan, I got you wrong! And I now stand one hundred percent behind your new reform policies. I thank you from the bottom of my heart, personally, and in the name of the people living in this country."

Everyone clapped and there was much backslapping, I even saw Brian sneaking in a hug with Jame Norton. I was deeply moved and felt like walking out the back door. Watching these powerful and emotional men talking with each other caused me to think back into the past, to the last time I had visited the girl with nine toes.

*B*e a shepherd
*N*ot one of the sheep

Chapter 29

I walked slowly along the ridge, Rick and his partner were following close behind me. I had told them both what I wanted to do and even though they were very suspicious, they agreed to wait for me on the jogging path. I found the place and slid down into the gully. I heard the silence and I could feel the intensity in the air as I came down to the river. Baldwa was not there to meet me–but I wasn't surprised. Walking out into the light I saw her sitting there on that same rock, with that same smile, with that same charisma of innocence and wisdom.

"Oh, Turawwa there you are, come to me, sit down, look at the river and notice the many currents flowing here and there. Much like your life turning around, moving against the stream, always in motion. Change your mind and change your life, as you have done in your quest to find your heart once again, to lead. You know, you haven't experienced anything new. You have also not gained any new wisdom. Your path was the everyday normal path of every human being on this planet. Many have wandered away from this path, others are still trying to find it, and many will never, ever find it. But the people who walk this path will change the world, sometimes in big ways, but also sometimes in small ways.

I will leave you soon and you will not see me again in your lifetime. But before we depart from each other I want to tell you a few more songlines so that you may meditate on them. Fear is just a four letter word and is not an emotion. Fear is only a figment of your imagination and is not the reality. So whatever happens in your future, look behind the fear and there you will find freedom. Believe in yourself and know the beauty within. You are a wonderful, shining star in the firmament of life. Show your light and allow the shadows to disappear. Love your fellow man as you love yourself, but at the same time always look for the darkness and confusion within his negative belief system, for this is not what he really is, this is only a collection of pain and insecurity experienced in the water of the past that flows beneath the bridges of knowledge connecting the past with the present. We can learn from our past mistakes– but only if we have the courage to open our eyes and hearts. You are now strong, Turawwa, and you *are* a leader who leads with the heart. But your lessons and challenges have not yet ended. They will only end at that time when you cross over into the dreamland. There will be times when you stand alone, not quite sure about which direction to take, you will rely on your vision, intuition, and body triggers. But even then–mistakes will you make. But these mistakes are the golden opportunities to walk further on the path of life. We know that all brothers and sisters are united, and that only envy and fear stands between war and world peace. *You*, in your lifetime, will see an earth free of mass destruction and racial prejudice–a planet that will be healed of global pollution and animal extinction. And we of the dreamtime will stand at the side of the other leaders of this world and teach them how to, *lead with the heart!*"

I could see the mist rising from the river swallowing up her small, black body, and the girl with nine toes left my life forever.

"John! John! Did you hear me? We all want to go outside into the park and watch the sun going down on this wonderful day . . . come on mate, let's go!"

The five men walked out of Parliament House onto the hill above the lake, and looking towards the direction where the sun was going down, they saw the red and orange, fire of the sun filling the sky with **Hope**.

Into your soul and way beyond

Our Prime Minister has done it again!

Changing the laws, governing the rights of our indigenous people. As of now every Aborigine has exactly the same rights as his white brother. Any person violating this right will be prosecuted. All lands connected with the spiritual beliefs of the Aborigines now belong to the aboriginal race and they alone will decide how it is to be used. It is interesting for us is to see the results of the Prime Minister's black and white integration programme. Which carries the belief that no Aborigine should ever be forced to live in a house or a city if he does not wish to. Areas outside major cities have been relegated to the Aborigines where they can live in their natural surroundings and at the same time be connected to the city. These areas are governed by the people themselves. At the same time it is now a part of the education programme of every child in Australia to live for three months with the Aborigines–experiencing their culture, the dreamtime legends and natural healing. This is only one part of the awesome change that has uplifted our country in recent times. Australia is proud of its son, Mr John Macmilan who carries the tribal name Turawwa and whose skin is also as black as the darkest night.

Walter Krikowa upi

The Beginning

Acknowledgements

First of all I would like to apologise to the indigenous people of Australia for the imaginative use of their language as well as the legends of the Dreamtime. My second apology goes to the Australian government. Some of the ministerial names as well as the workings of parliament and how the prime minister lives and works are figments of my imagination. Special thanks go to Tom Garvey (not the lawyer mentioned in this book) for his proof reading, and also to Elise Pomier. A big thanks to Raven Brooks for the final editing. Thank you Tony, my friend, for the wonderful foreword that you wrote for this story. I also want to thank Ute und Emil, for their love, and for being an important part of my life. As always many thanks to my partner Cordula for supporting me in writing this book, and for her inspiration and neverending love. Thanks also go, of course, to the girl with nine toes, without her, this book would never have been written – give our love to Max.

Ray Wilkins FRSA grew up in Australia where he first experienced the Aboriginal culture. He has lived and worked in England, Switzerland, Crete, India and Germany. He now lives in Belgium, on a working farm in the country, together with his partner and many animals. He is a professional coach, trainer, artist, practitioner of natural medicine, and songwriter.

He runs the international College for coaching, training, art and complementary medicine, "The Barefoot School," together with his partner Cordula Ehms. This is his first novel.

His websites:
www.thebarefootschool.com
www.song-rays.com

Follow your heart